It's another Quality Book from CGP

This book is for anyone doing Edexcel IGCSE Mathematics (Specification A).

It contains lots of tricky questions designed
to make you sweat — because that's the only
way you'll get any better.

It's also got some daft bits in to try and make
the whole experience at least vaguely
entertaining for you.

What CGP is all about

Our sole aim here at CGP is to produce the highest quality
books — carefully written, immaculately presented and
dangerously close to being funny.

Then we work our socks off to get them out to you
— at the cheapest possible prices.

Contents

Section Five

SHAPES, VECTORS AND TRANSFORMATIONS

Section Six

GEOMETRY

Section Seven

STATISTICS

Throughout this book, the more challenging questions are marked like this **Q1**.

Published by CGP

Illustrated by Ruso Bradley, Lex Ward and Ashley Tyson

From original material by Richard Parsons.

Contributors:
Gill Allen, JE Dodds, Sally Gill, Mark Haslam, C McLoughlin, John Waller, Dave Williams

Updated by:
Helena Hayes, Paul Jordin, Sharon Keeley-Holden, Adam Moorhouse

With thanks to Glenn Rogers and James Welham for the proofreading.

ISBN: 978 1 84762 555 7

Groovy website: www.cgpbooks.co.uk
Printed by Elanders Ltd, Newcastle upon Tyne.
Jolly bits of clipart from CorelDRAW® and VECTOR.

Photocopying — it's dull, it takes ages... and sometimes it's a bit naughty. Luckily, it's dead cheap, easy and quick to order more copies of this book from CGP — just call us on 0870 750 1242. Phew!

Text, design, layout and original illustrations © Richard Parsons 2010
All rights reserved.

Multiples, Factors and Primes

Q1   1   3   6   9   12
From the numbers above, write down:
   a) a multiple of 4
   b) the prime number
   c) two square numbers
   d) three factors of 27
   e) two numbers, P and Q, that satisfy both P = 2Q and P = $\sqrt{144}$

This is real basic stuff —
you just have to know
your times tables. And
your primes, of course...

Q2   48 students went on a geography field trip.
Their teachers split them into equal groups.
Suggest five different ways that the teachers
might have split up the students.

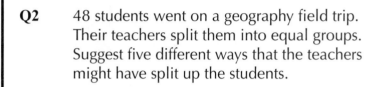

Q3   A school ran 3 evening classes: Conversational French, Cake Making and Woodturning.
The Conversational French class had 29 students, Cake Making had 27 students, and the
Woodturning class had 23. For which classes did the teacher have difficulty dividing the
students into equal groups?

Q4 **a)** Write down the first five cube numbers.
   b) Which of the numbers given in part **a)** are multiples of 2?
   c) Which of the numbers given in part **a)** are multiples of 3?
   d) Which of the numbers given in part **a)** are multiples of 4?
   e) Which of the numbers given in part **a)** are multiples of 5?

Q5   Express the following as products of powers of prime factors:
   a) 18
   b) 140
   c) 47

The tricky bit is remembering that a <u>prime factorisation</u>
includes <u>all</u> the prime factors that multiply to make that
number — so you've got to repeat some of them.

Q6 **a)** List the first five prime numbers.
   b) If added together, what is their total?
   c) Write down the prime factorisation of the answer to part **b)**.

Q7 **a)** List the first five odd numbers.
   b) If added together, what is their total?
   c) Write down the prime factorisation of the answer to part **b)**.

Multiples, Factors and Primes

Q8 The prime factorisation of a certain number is $3^2 \times 5 \times 11$.
  a) Write down the number.
  b) Write down the prime factorisation of 165.

Q9 The first ten triangle numbers are:

  1, 3, 6, 10, 15, 21, 28, 36, 45, 55

  a) From the list pick out all the multiples of 2.
  b) From the list pick out all the multiples of 3.
  c) From the list pick out any prime numbers.
  d) Add the numbers in the list together and write
     down the prime factorisation of the total.

Q10 Gordon is doing some woodwork and needs to calculate
  the volume of a wooden rectangular block (a cuboid).
  The length of the block is 50 cm, the height 25 cm and the width 16 cm.
  a) What is the volume (in cm³) of the wooden block?
  b) What is the prime factorisation of the number found in part **a)**?
  c) Gordon needs to cut the block into smaller blocks with dimensions 4 cm × 5 cm × 5 cm.
     What is the maximum number of small blocks Gordon can make from the larger block?
     Make sure you show all your working.

Q11 The prime factorisation of a certain number is $2^3 \times 5 \times 17$.
  a) What is the number?
  b) What is the prime factorisation of half of this number?
  c) What is the prime factorisation of a quarter of the number?
  d) What is the prime factorisation of an eighth of the number?

Q12 Bryan and Sue were playing a guessing game. Sue thought of a number
  between 1 and 100 which Bryan had to guess. Bryan was allowed to ask five
  questions, which are listed with Sue's responses in the table below.

Bryan's Questions	Sue's Responses
Is it prime?	No
Is it odd?	No
Is it less than 50?	Yes
Is it a multiple of 3?	Yes
Is it a multiple of 7?	Yes

Start by writing down
a number table up to 100.
Look at each response in
turn and cross off numbers
until you've only got
one left.

  What is the number that Sue thought of?

LCM and HCF

These two fancy names always put people off — but really they're dead easy. Just learn these simple facts:

1) The Lowest Common Multiple (LCM) is the SMALLEST number that will DIVIDE BY ALL the numbers in question.

E.g. 3, 6, 9, 12, 15 are all multiples of 3.
5, 10, 15, 20, 25 are all multiples of 5.
The lowest number that is in both lists is 15, so 15 is the LCM of 3 and 5.

2) The Highest Common Factor (HCF) is the BIGGEST number that will DIVIDE INTO ALL the numbers in question.

E.g. 1, 2, 4, 8 are all factors of 8.
1, 2, 3, 4, 6, 12 are all factors of 12.
The highest number that is in both lists is 4, so 4 is the HCF of 8 and 12.

Q1 a) List the first ten multiples of 6, starting at 6.
b) List the first ten multiples of 5, starting at 5.
c) What is the LCM of 5 and 6?

I tell you what, it's a lot easier to find the LCM or HCF once you've listed the multiples or factors. If you miss out this step it'll all go horribly wrong, believe me.

Q2 a) List all the factors of 30.
b) List all the factors of 48.
c) What is the HCF of 30 and 48?

Q3 For each set of numbers find the HCF.
a) 40, 60
b) 10, 40, 60
c) 10, 24, 40, 60
d) 15, 45
e) 15, 30, 45
f) 15, 20, 30, 45
g) 32, 64
h) 32, 48, 64
i) 16, 32, 48, 64

Q4 For each set of numbers find the LCM.
a) 40, 60
b) 10, 40, 60
c) 10, 24, 40, 60
d) 15, 45
e) 15, 30, 45
f) 15, 20, 30, 45
g) 32, 64
h) 32, 48, 64
i) 16, 32, 48, 64

Q5 Lars, Rita and Alan regularly go swimming. Lars goes every 2 days, Rita goes every 3 days and Alan goes every 5 days. They all went swimming together on Friday 1st June.

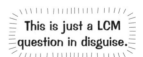

This is just a LCM question in disguise.

a) On what date will Lars and Rita next go swimming together?
b) On what date will Rita and Alan next go swimming together?
c) On what day of the week will all 3 next go swimming together?
d) Which of the 3 (if any) will go swimming on 15th June?

SECTION ONE — NUMBERS

Fractions, Decimals and Percentages

I reckon that converting decimals to percentages is about as easy as it gets — so make the most of it.

Q1 Express each of the following as a percentage:

a) 0.25　　c) 0.75　　e) 0.4152　　g) 0.3962

b) 0.5　　　d) 0.1　　　f) 0.8406　　h) 0.2828

> All you're doing is multiplying by 100 — it really couldn't be easier.

Q2 Express each percentage as a decimal:

a) 50%　　c) 40%　　e) 60.2%　　g) 43.1%

b) 12%　　d) 34%　　f) 54.9%　　h) 78.8%

> Now you're dividing by 100 — so just move the decimal point to the left.

Q3 Express each of the following as a percentage. Round your answers to 1 d.p. where necessary.

a) $\dfrac{1}{2}$　　　　　　e) $\dfrac{1}{25}$

b) $\dfrac{1}{4}$　　　　　　f) $\dfrac{2}{3}$

c) $\dfrac{1}{8}$　　　　　　g) $\dfrac{4}{15}$

d) $\dfrac{3}{4}$　　　　　　h) $\dfrac{2}{7}$

Q4 Express each percentage as a fraction in its lowest terms:

a) 25%　　e) 8.2%

b) 60%　　f) 49.6%

c) 45%　　g) 88.6%

d) 30%　　h) 32.4%

> Best thing to do with e)-h) is to put them over 100, then get rid of the decimal point by multiplying top and bottom by 10. Then just cancel down as normal.

Q5 119 out of 140 houses on an estate have DVD players. What percentage is this?

Q6 In an exam Tina scored 52/80. The grade she receives depends on the percentage scored. What grade will Tina get?

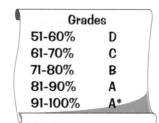

Grades	
51-60%	D
61-70%	C
71-80%	B
81-90%	A
91-100%	A*

Fractions, Decimals and Percentages

 <u>Decimals</u> are just another way of writing <u>fractions</u> —
so it's easy to convert between the two...

Q7 Without using a calculator, write the following fractions as decimals:

a) $\dfrac{3}{10}$ c) $\dfrac{2}{5}$ e) $\dfrac{14}{8}$ g) $\dfrac{24}{40}$

b) $\dfrac{37}{100}$ d) $\dfrac{3}{8}$ f) $\dfrac{8}{64}$ h) $\dfrac{4}{80}$

Q8 Fill in the gaps in the following conversion table:

Fraction	Decimal
½	0.5
⅕	0.2
	0.125
	1.6
⁴⁄₁₆	
⁷⁄₂	
	0.x
ˣ⁄₁₀₀	
³⁄₂₀	
	0.45

$\dfrac{125}{1000}$

Q9 Write the following fractions as recurring decimals:

a) $\dfrac{5}{6}$ c) $\dfrac{7}{11}$ e) $\dfrac{10}{11}$ g) $\dfrac{478}{999}$

b) $\dfrac{7}{9}$ d) $\dfrac{47}{99}$ f) $\dfrac{29}{63}$ h) $\dfrac{5891}{9999}$

Q10 Write the following decimals as fractions in their lowest form:

a) 0.6 c) 0.95 e) 0.$\dot{3}$ g) 0.$\dot{1}$

b) 0.75 d) 0.128 f) 0.$\dot{6}$ h) 0.1$\dot{6}$

Q11 Write the following recurring decimals as fractions in their lowest form:

a) 0.222... c) 0.888... e) 0.121212... g) 0.753753753...

b) 0.444... d) 0.808080... f) 0.545545545... h) 0.156156156...

Fractions

Answer the following questions without using a calculator.

Q1 Carry out the following multiplications, giving your answers in their lowest terms:

a) $\frac{1}{8} \times \frac{1}{8} = \frac{1}{64}$

c) $\frac{3}{18} \times \frac{1}{3} = \frac{3}{54}$

e) $1\frac{1}{4} \times 4\frac{1}{8}$

b) $\frac{2}{3} \times \frac{1}{6} = \frac{2}{18}$

d) $1\frac{1}{4} \times 3\frac{1}{8}$

f) $\frac{9}{10} \times \frac{9}{100} \times \frac{1}{100}$

$\frac{5}{4} \times \frac{25}{8} = \frac{225}{32}$

Q2 Carry out the following divisions, giving your answers in their lowest terms:

a) $\frac{1}{8} \div \frac{1}{8}$

c) $\frac{3}{18} \div \frac{1}{3}$

e) $1\frac{1}{4} \div 4\frac{1}{8}$

b) $\frac{2}{3} \div \frac{1}{6}$

d) $1\frac{1}{4} \div 3\frac{1}{8}$

f) $\left(\frac{9}{10} \div \frac{9}{100}\right) \div \frac{1}{100}$

Q3 Evaluate the following, giving your answers in their lowest terms:

a) $\frac{1}{8} + \frac{1}{8}$

c) $\frac{3}{18} + \frac{1}{3}$

e) $1\frac{1}{4} + 4\frac{1}{8}$

b) $\frac{1}{6} + \frac{2}{3}$

d) $1\frac{1}{4} + 3\frac{1}{8}$

f) $\frac{9}{10} + \frac{9}{100} + \frac{1}{100}$

Q4 Caley is making some punch for her birthday party. She mixes $\frac{1}{2}$ litre of cranberry juice, $1\frac{1}{2}$ litres of apple juice, $\frac{2}{3}$ litre of orange juice and $\frac{4}{5}$ litre of pineapple juice. She has a bowl that will hold 4 litres. Will this be big enough to contain all of the punch?

Q5 Evaluate the following, giving your answers in their lowest terms:

a) $\frac{1}{8} - \frac{1}{8}$

c) $\frac{3}{18} - \frac{1}{3}$

e) $1\frac{1}{4} - 4\frac{1}{8}$

b) $\frac{2}{3} - \frac{1}{6}$

d) $3\frac{1}{8} - 1\frac{1}{4}$

f) $\left(\frac{9}{10} - \frac{9}{100}\right) - \frac{1}{100}$

Q6 Evaluate the following, giving your answers in their lowest terms:

a) $\frac{1}{2} + \frac{1}{4}$

e) $6 \times \frac{2}{3}$

i) $3 + \frac{8}{5}$

b) $\frac{2}{3} - \frac{1}{4}$

f) $\frac{4}{5} \div \frac{2}{3}$

j) $\frac{2}{3}\left(\frac{3}{4} + \frac{4}{5}\right)$

c) $\frac{1}{5} + \frac{2}{3} - \frac{2}{5}$

g) $\frac{5}{12} \times \frac{3}{2}$

k) $\left(\frac{1}{7} + \frac{3}{14}\right) \times \left(3 - \frac{1}{5}\right)$

d) $5 - \frac{1}{4}$

h) $\frac{5}{6} - \frac{7}{8}$

l) $\left(\frac{3}{4} - \frac{1}{5}\right) \div \left(\frac{7}{8} + \frac{1}{16}\right)$

Fractions

The cunning bit with long wordy questions is picking out the important bits and then translating them into numbers. It's not that easy at first, but you'll get better — I guess you've just gotta learn to ignore the waffly stuff.

Answer these without using your calculator:

Q7 What fraction of 1 hour is:
a) 5 minutes
b) 15 minutes
c) 40 minutes?

Q8 If a TV programme lasts 40 minutes, what fraction of the programme is left after:
a) 10 minutes
b) 15 minutes
c) 35 minutes?

Q9 A café employs eighteen girls and twelve boys to wait at tables. Another six boys and nine girls work in the kitchen.
What fraction of the <u>kitchen staff</u> are girls?
What fraction of the <u>employees</u> are boys?

Q10

In a survey, people were asked if they liked a new cola drink. One in five thought it was great, four out of fifteen felt there was no difference in taste, three in ten disliked it and <u>the rest</u> offered no opinion.
What fraction of people offered no opinion?

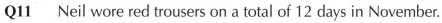

Forget all about cola drinks — just write it all as a sum, then do the calculation. Nowt to it.

Q11 Neil wore red trousers on a total of 12 days in November.
a) On what fraction of the total number of days in November did Neil wear <u>red trousers</u>?
b) For 1/5 of the days in November Neil wore a <u>blue shirt</u>. How many days is this?

Q12

The Sandwich Club of Great Britain are going on their annual picnic.
a) The boxes they use to transport their sandwiches are 10 inches high and are the width and length of a single sandwich. Each sandwich is 5/8 inch thick. How many boxes will they need for 80 sandwiches?
b) How tall would the box need to be if <u>40</u> sandwiches were to be stacked inside?

Fractions

You can use your calculator for these.

Q13 The population of Australia is 18 million, of which 3.5 million people live in Sydney and 1 million people live in Perth.

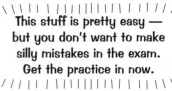

This stuff is pretty easy — but you don't want to make silly mistakes in the exam. Get the practice in now.

   a) What fraction of the population live in Perth?
   b) What fraction of the population live in Perth or Sydney?

Q14 Green Island is split into six regions A, B, C, D, E and F. The areas of the six regions are 12, 2, 3, 18, 4 and 9 km² respectively.
   a) What is the total area of the island?
   b) What fraction of the island's area is taken up by the two largest regions?

Q15 In a consumer survey, 100 people stated their favourite vegetable. 25 people chose peas, 35 carrots and 32 runner beans.
   a) How many of the 100 people chose a vegetable other than peas, carrots or runner beans?
   b) What fraction of the 100 people chose carrots as their favourite vegetable?
   c) What fraction of the 100 people chose peas as their favourite vegetable?
   d) At least how many people chose a green vegetable as their favourite?
   e) Not more than how many people chose a green vegetable as their favourite?

Q16 A ball is dropped from a height of 6 m.

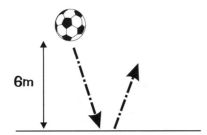

6m

After each bounce the ball rises to 2/3 of its previous height. What height will it reach after the third bounce?

Q17 George wants to make a cake. The recipe requires 150 g each of flour, sugar and butter, and 3 eggs. George only has 2 eggs so he decides to make a smaller cake with the same proportions.
   a) How much flour will George need to use?
   b) If each egg weighs 25 g, how much will the cake weigh before it goes in the oven?
   c) What fraction of the uncooked weight is flour?
   d) If the cake loses 1/7 of its weight during baking (due to moisture loss) what will it weigh after baking?

Q18 Jenny goes shopping. She gets 1/3 off a bag priced £28, 1/5 off a dress priced £62 and 2/3 off a hat priced £14. How much money does she save?

Ratios

 I don't want to spoil the surprise, but you're going to need your calculator for this bit — get your finger on that fraction button...

RATIOS are like FRACTIONS which are like DECIMALS

We can treat the RATIO 3:4 like the FRACTION ¾, which is 0.75 as a DECIMAL.

Watch out though — this <u>isn't</u> ¾ of the <u>total</u>:

If there are girls and boys in the ratio **3:4**, it means there's ¾ as many girls as boys.

So if there's 8 boys, there's ¾ × 8 = 6 girls.

Q1 Write these ratios in their simplest forms:
- **a)** 6:8
- **b)** 5:20
- **c)** 1.5:3
- **d)** 2¼:4
- **e)** 2 weeks:4 days
- **f)** £1.26:14p

Q2 A rectangle has sides in the ratio 1:2. Calculate the length of the longer side if the shorter side is:
- **a)** 3 cm
- **b)** 5.5 cm
- **c)** 15.2 m

Calculate the length of the shorter side if the longer side is:
- **d)** 3 cm
- **e)** 5.5 cm
- **f)** 15.2 m

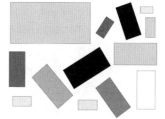

Q3 Divide the following amounts in the ratios given:
- **a)** £20 in the ratio 2:3
- **b)** 150 m in the ratio 8:7
- **c)** 500 g in the ratio 1:2:2
- **d)** 8 hrs in the ratio 1:2:3

For these you add up the ratio numbers to find the total number of parts and <u>divide</u> by this. Then <u>multiply</u> by each number in the ratio separately to find the different amounts.

Q4 **a)** <u>Increase</u> £3.20 in the ratio 2:3.
b) <u>Decrease</u> 120 cm in the ratio 3:2.

Q5 John and Peter share a bar of chocolate marked into 16 squares. They share it in the ratio 1:3 respectively. How many squares does each boy get?

Q6  A 2 litre bottle of cola is to be shared between three girls in the ratio 2:3:5. How many <u>millilitres</u> will each girl get?

 <u>Watch out for your units</u> — you'll have to change them over for this one — and your answer should be in <u>millilitres</u>.

Q7 Oak and ash saplings are planted along a roadside in the ratio 2:3 respectively. If there are 20 oak saplings, how many ash saplings are there?

Q8 Tony gives £100 to be shared by Jane, Holly and Rosemary in a ratio according to their <u>age</u>. Jane is 10, Holly is 12 and Rosemary is 3 years old. How much will each child get?

Q9 Sunil and Paul work in a restaurant. As they work different hours, they split their tips in the ratio 3:4. One night they got £28 in tips between them. Who got the most money from the tips and how much did they get?

Ratios

Q10 The recipe for flapjacks is 250 g of oats, 150 g of brown sugar and 100 g of margarine. What <u>fraction of the mixture</u> is:

a) oats?

b) sugar?

Q11 The ratio of girls to boys in a school is 7:6. If there are 455 pupils in total, how many are

a) girls?

b) boys?

Q12 Sarah works as a waitress. Each week, she splits her wage into spending money and savings in the ratio 7:3.

a) One week, Sarah earns £130. How much should she put in her savings that week?

b) The next week, Sarah put £42 into her savings. How much did she earn in total that week?

Q13 An architect is drawing the plan of a house to a scale of 1 cm to 3 m.

a) Write this ratio in its simplest form.

b) How wide is a room that appears as 2 cm on the drawing?

c) The hall is 10 m long. How long will the architect need to make it on the drawing?

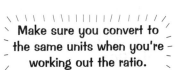

Make sure you convert to the same units when you're working out the ratio.

Q14 Concrete is mixed using cement, sand and gravel in the ratio 1:3:6. If Dave uses a 5 kg bag of cement, how much:

a) sand does he need?

b) gravel does he need?

c) If Dave needs 80 kg of concrete, how much of each substance does he need?

Q15

I picked some strawberries after a few wet days. Some were nibbled by snails, some were mouldy and some fine. The ratio was 2:3:10 respectively. If <u>9 strawberries were mouldy</u> how many:

a) were fine?

b) were not fine?

c) What fraction of the total amount were fine?

Q16 Salt & Vinegar, Cheese & Onion and Prawn Cocktail flavour crisps were sold in the school tuck shop in <u>the ratio 5:3:2</u>. If 18 bags of Prawn Cocktail were sold, how many bags:

a) of Salt & Vinegar were sold?

b) were sold altogether?

SECTION ONE — NUMBERS

Proportion

Q1   If 3 minibuses can carry 51 students, how many students can 5 minibuses carry? $=77$

Q2   If 17 textbooks cost £150.45, how much will 28 cost? $=£247.80$

Q3   If it takes 4 people 28 hours to complete a task, how long would it take just one person?   7

Q4   A person earns £6.20 an hour. How much do they earn for 15½ hours work?

Q5   Wool from 8 sheep is needed to make a scarf.
How many are needed to make 12 scarves?

Q6   On a map, 2 cm represents 3 km.
    a) If two towns are 14 km apart, what is the distance between them on the map?
    b) If two road junctions are 20.3 cm apart on the map, what is their real distance apart?

Q7   A herd of 7 cows produces 161 litres of milk a day.
Find the smallest number of cows it would take to
produce at least 1000 litres per day.

Q8   The number of people who have their hearing damaged at a concert is proportional to
how loud it is. 480 people have their hearing damaged when the volume is set at '6'.
How many people suffer hearing damage when:
    a) the volume is set at '4'?
    b) the volume is set at '7'?
    c) the volume is turned up to '11'?

Q9   A scientist proposes that rainfall is proportional to latitude.
It rains an average of 53.1 cm a year in Milton Keynes,
which is at latitude 52.0° N. If the scientist is correct,
what is the average rainfall in:
    a) Ulverston — latitude 54.2° N?
    b) Boscastle — latitude 50.4° N?
       If average daytime temperature in July is inversely
       proportional to latitude and it's 21.0 °C in Boscastle,
       what will the average daytime temperature in July be in:
    c) Milton Keynes?
    d) Ulverston?

Q10   The speed of light is inversely proportional to the
'refractive index' of the material it's travelling through.
The speed of light in water is 225 000 km/s. Water has a refractive index of 1.33.
What is the speed of light in:
    a) Glass which has a refractive index of 1.50?
    b) Diamond which has a refractive index of 2.42?
    c) A vacuum which has a refractive index of 1.00?

Percentages

Make sure you can switch from fractions to decimals to percentages before you start.

Q1   Express each percentage as a decimal:

a) 20%   **b)** 35%   **c)** 2%   **d)** 62.5%

Q2   Express each percentage as a fraction in its lowest terms:

a) 20%   **b)** 3%   **c)** 70%   **d)** 84.2%

Q3   Express each of the following as a percentage:

a) $\frac{1}{8}$ **b)** 0.23   **c)** $\frac{12}{40}$ **d)** 0.34

Q4   In a French test, Lauren scored 17/20. What percentage is this?

Q5   87 out of 120 pupils at Backwater School have access to a computer.
           What percentage is this?

**There are three types of percentage question. The first one is working out
"something % of something else" — it's dead easy. Just remember to
add it back on to the original amount if you've got a VAT question.**

Q6   John bought a new TV. The tag in the shop said it cost £299 + VAT.
           If VAT is charged at 17½%, how much did he pay (to the nearest penny)?

Q7    Four friends stay at the Pickled Parrot Hotel for a night and each
           have an evening meal. Bed and Breakfast costs £37 per person and
           the evening meal costs £15 per person. How much is the total cost,
           if VAT is added at 17½%?

Q8   The owners of a museum are expecting a 14% increase in visitors next year.
           This year they had 20 200 visitors.
           How many visitors should they expect next year?

Percentages

Q9 Donald earns an annual wage of £23,500. He doesn't pay tax on the first £6,400 that he earns. How much income tax does he pay a year if the rate of tax is:
a) 25%
b) 40%?

Q10 Tim is choosing between two cars to buy.
The first car is priced at £8495 and has 15% off. *7220.75*
The second car is priced at £8195 and has 12% off. *982 7211.6*
Which car is the cheapest? Show your working.

Q11 Tanya paid £6500 for her new car. Each year its value decreased by 8%.
a) How much was it worth when it was one year old? *5980*
b) How much was it worth when it was two years old? *5460*

Q12 Jeremy wanted a new sofa for his lounge. A local furniture shop had just what he was looking for — and for only £130.00 + VAT. Jeremy had £150 pounds in his bank account. If VAT was charged at 17½%, could Jeremy afford the sofa?

Here's the 2ⁿᵈ type — finding "something <u>as a percentage</u> of something else" — in this case you're looking at percentage <u>change</u>, so don't forget to find the difference in values first.

Q13 During a rainstorm, a water butt increased in weight from 10.4 kg to 13.6 kg. What was the percentage increase (to the nearest per cent)?

Q14 An electrical store reduces the price of a particular camera from £90.00 to £78.30. What is the percentage reduction?

Q15 There are approximately 6000 fish and chip shops in the UK. On average, a fish and chip shop gets about 160 visitors each day. Given that the population of the UK is roughly 60 million, approximately what percentage of the population visit a fish and chip shop each day?

Q16 At birth, Veronica was 0.3 m tall. By adulthood she had grown to 1.5 m tall. Calculate her height now as a percentage of her height at birth.

Percentages

Q17 Desmond's maths exam is next week. As part of his revision he attempted 31 questions on his least favourite topic of percentages. He got 21 questions right on the first attempt. Two days later he tried all 31 questions again and this time got 29 correct.

    a) What percentage of questions did he get correct on his first attempt?

    b) What percentage of questions did he get correct on his second attempt?

    c) What is the percentage increase in the number of questions Desmond got right?

Q18 I wish to invest £1000 for a period of three years and have decided to place my money with the Highrise Building Society on 1 January. If I choose to use the Gold Account I will withdraw the interest at the end of each year. If I choose to use the Silver Account I will leave the interest to be added to the capital at the end of each year.

Highrise Building Society

Gold Account	7.875% p.a
Silver Account	7.00% p.a

    a) Calculate the total interest I will receive if I use the Gold Account.

    b) Calculate the total interest I will receive if I use the Silver Account.

After some thought I decide to use the Gold Account and leave the interest to be added to the capital at the end of each year.

    c) Calculate the total interest I will now receive from the Gold Account.

Q19 If $L = MN$, what is the percentage increase in L if M increases by 15% and N increases by 20%?

Q20 An electrical shop buys a stereo from a wholesaler for £x and increases its price by 35% to make a profit. When the stereo doesn't sell, the shop reduces its price by 20%. If the stereo now sells, calculate the shop's overall percentage profit.

Q21 A couple bought their house 2 years ago for £y. In the first year, house prices in their area rose by 10%. In the second year, house prices in their area fell by 5%. Calculate the percentage profit they would make if they sold their house now.

Ooh... here's the 3rd type — finding the <u>original value</u>. The bit most people get wrong is deciding whether the value given represents <u>more</u> or <u>less than 100%</u> of the original — so <u>always</u> check your answer <u>makes sense</u>.

Q22 In the new year sales Robin bought a tennis racket for £68.00. The original price had been reduced by 15%. What was the original price?

Q23 There are 360 people living in a certain village. The population of the village has grown by 20% over the past year.

    a) How many people lived in the village one year ago?

    b) If the village continues to grow at the same rate, how many whole years from today will it be before the population is more than twice its current size?

Interest

You may not have a lot of interest in this page,
but it will be useful to invest some time in it. Ah-ha!

Q1 A financial advisor is asked to calculate the future value of his clients' investments.
Calculate the amount in each of these accounts if:
a) £200 is invested for 10 years at 9% compound interest per annum
b) £500 is invested for 3 years at 7% compound interest per annum
c) £750 is invested for 6 months at 8% compound interest per annum
d) £1000 is invested for 12 months at 6.5% compound interest per annum.

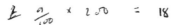

Q2 Mrs Smith decides to invest £7000 in a savings account. She has the choice of putting
all her money into an account paying 5% compound interest per annum or she can put
half of her investment into an account paying 6% compound interest per annum and the
remaining half into an account paying 4% compound interest per annum.
If she left the investment alone for 3 years, which is her best option and by how much?

Q3 A used car salesman is buying stock at an auction. Before the auction, he estimates
the value of each car on offer using their original price, their age, and a depreciation of
14% each year. This value is the maximum amount he will bid for each car.
Calculate the maximum amount he should bid on these used cars:
a) a car which cost £8495 six months ago
b) a car which cost £34 000 eighteen months ago
c) a car which cost £13 495 two years ago
d) a car which cost £14 395 two years ago
e) a car which cost £11 295 three years ago
f) a car which cost £6795 twelve months ago.

Q4 Julia is opening a bank account. There are three options available — an account that
pays 4% compound interest per year, an account that pays 5% simple interest per year
and an account that pays £5 per month. Which should she choose if she invests:
a) £1000 for 1 year?
b) £3000 for 10 years?
c) £2200 for 25 years?
Show your workings for each answer.

I'd put my money in
Victorian rolling pins, myself...

Q5 An accountant is looking at some financial records. She needs to work out the principal
amount that was invested a year ago. What was the principal amount invested in:
a) an account containing £278.10 that paid 3% interest?
b) an account containing £837.40 that paid 6% interest?
c) an account containing £1175.20 that paid 4% interest?
d) shares that are worth £8172.24 and have increased in value by 2%?
e) shares that are worth £5049 and have decreased in value by 1%?

SECTION TWO — MORE NUMBERS

Square Roots and Cube Roots

Square root just means "WHAT NUMBER TIMES ITSELF (e.g. 2×2) GIVES..."
The square roots of 64 are 8 and –8 because 8×8=64 and -8×-8=64.

Cube root means "WHAT NUMBER TIMES ITSELF TWICE (e.g. 2×2×2) GIVES ..."
The cube root of 27 is 3 because 3×3×3=27.

Square roots always have a + and – answer, cube roots only have 1 answer.   Tip

Q1 Use the $\sqrt{}$ button on your calculator to find the following <u>positive</u> square roots to 1 d.p.

a) $\sqrt{60}$ e) $\sqrt{520}$ i) $\sqrt{170}$

b) $\sqrt{19}$ f) $\sqrt{75}$ j) $\sqrt{7220}$

c) $\sqrt{34}$ g) $\sqrt{750}$ k) $\sqrt{1\,000\,050}$

d) $\sqrt{200}$ h) $\sqrt{0.9}$ l) $\sqrt{27}$

Q2 Without using a calculator, write down both answers to each of the following:

a) $\sqrt{4}$ d) $\sqrt{49}$ g) $\sqrt{144}$

b) $\sqrt{16}$ e) $\sqrt{25}$ h) $\sqrt{64}$

c) $\sqrt{9}$ f) $\sqrt{100}$ i) $\sqrt{81}$

Q3 Use your calculator to find the following:

a) $\sqrt[3]{4096}$ c) $\sqrt[3]{1331}$ e) $\sqrt[3]{1}$

b) $\sqrt[3]{1728}$ d) $\sqrt[3]{1\,000\,000}$ f) $\sqrt[3]{0.125}$

Q4 Without using a calculator, find the value of the following:

a) $\sqrt[3]{64}$ c) $\sqrt[3]{125}$ e) $\sqrt[3]{216}$

b) $\sqrt[3]{512}$ d) $\sqrt[3]{1000}$ f) $\sqrt[3]{8000}$

Q5 Nida is buying a small storage box online. She sees a cube box with a volume of 343 cm³. What is the length of each box edge?

Q6 A farmer is buying fencing to surround a square field of area 3600 m². What length of fencing does he need to buy?

Q7 Sarah thinks of a number. She calculates that the square of the number is 256. What is the square root of the number?

Manipulating Surds

Q1 Simplify:

Remember — $\sqrt{a} \times \sqrt{b} = \sqrt{(ab)}$.

a) $\sqrt{2} \times \sqrt{2}$

d) $\left(\dfrac{\sqrt{2}}{\sqrt{3}}\right)^2$

g) $\sqrt{4} - \sqrt{1}$

j) $\sqrt{x^2}$

b) $\dfrac{\sqrt{2}}{\sqrt{1}}$

e) $\sqrt{5} \times \sqrt{3}$

h) $\left(\dfrac{\sqrt{5}}{\sqrt{2}}\right)^2$

k) $\sqrt{8} \times \sqrt{8}$

c) $\dfrac{\sqrt{3}}{\sqrt{3}}$

f) $\dfrac{\sqrt{20}}{\sqrt{5}}$

i) $(\sqrt{x})^2$

l) $\sqrt{18} - \sqrt{9}$

Q2 Simplify:

a) $(2 + \sqrt{5})^2$

b) $(5 + \sqrt{6})^2$

c) $(2 + \sqrt{3})(2 - \sqrt{3})$

Q3 A farmer has a square pig pen with an area of 17 m². Find the exact length of each of the pen's sides.

Q4 Rationalise the denominators of the following expressions, and then simplify if necessary.

a) $\dfrac{1}{\sqrt{2}}$

c) $\dfrac{a}{\frac{\sqrt{40}}{2}}$

e) $\dfrac{1}{1 + \sqrt{2}}$

g) $\dfrac{2}{1 + \sqrt{6}}$

b) $\dfrac{2}{\sqrt{8}}$

d) $\dfrac{x}{\sqrt{xy}}$

f) $\dfrac{6}{3 + \sqrt{3}}$

h) $\dfrac{5 + \sqrt{5}}{5 - \sqrt{5}}$

Remember: rationalising the denominator means getting rid of the square root signs on the bottom of fractions.

Q5 Express $\dfrac{9}{\sqrt{3}}$ in the form $a\sqrt{3}$.

Q6 Express $\sqrt{32} + 3\sqrt{2}$ in the form $a\sqrt{2}$.

Q7 Express $(1 + 3\sqrt{2})^2$ in the form $a + b\sqrt{2}$.

Powers and Roots

Hang on there. Before you try this page, make sure you know all
the rules for dealing with powers...

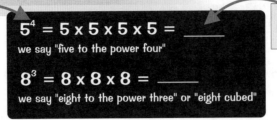

$5^4 = 5 \times 5 \times 5 \times 5 = $ _____

we say "five to the power four"

$8^3 = 8 \times 8 \times 8 = $ _____

we say "eight to the power three" or "eight cubed"

The small number
is called the <u>power</u>
or <u>index number</u>.
Remember the plural
of index is <u>indices</u>.

To save time try using the power button
on your calculator

e.g.

Q1 Complete the following:
a) $2^4 = 2 \times 2 \times 2 \times 2$ =
b) $10^3 = 10 \times 10 \times 10$ =
c) $3^5 = 3 \times ...$ =
d) $4^6 = 4 \times ...$ =
e) $1^9 = 1 \times ...$ =
f) $5^6 = 5 \times ...$ =

Q2 Simplify the following:
a) $2 \times 2 \times 2 \times 2 \times 2 \times 2 \times 2 \times 2$
b) $12 \times 12 \times 12 \times 12 \times 12$
c) $x \times x \times x \times x \times x \times x$
d) $m \times m \times m$
e) $y \times y \times y \times y$
f) $z \times z \times z \times z \times z \times z$

Q3 Complete the following (the first one has been done for you):
a) $10^2 \times 10^3 = (10 \times 10) \times (10 \times 10 \times 10)$ = 10^5
b) $10^3 \times 10^4 =$ =
c) $10^4 \times 10^2 =$ =
d) $10^5 \times 10^3 =$ =
e) What is the <u>quick method</u> for writing down the final result in **b)**, **c)** and **d)**?

Easy — you'll have learnt this from your power rules.

Q4 Complete the following (the first one has been done for you):
a) $2^4 \div 2^2 = \dfrac{(2 \times 2 \times 2 \times 2)}{(2 \times 2)} = 2^2$
c) $4^5 \div 4^3 = \dfrac{(4 \times 4 \times 4 \times 4 \times 4)}{} =$
b) $2^5 \div 2^2 = \dfrac{(2 \times 2 \times 2 \times 2 \times 2)}{(2 \times 2)} =$
d) $8^5 \div 8^2 =$ =

e) What is the quick method for writing down the final result in **b)**, **c)** and **d)**?

Q5 Which of the following are <u>true</u>?
a) $2^4 \times 2^6 = 2^{10}$
b) $2^2 \times 2^3 \times 2^4 = 2^9$
c) $2^3 \times 2^2 = 2^6$
d) $4^{10} \times 4^4 \times 4^2 = 4^{18}$
e) $2^1 \times 2^3 \times 2^4 = 2^8$
f) $10^4 \times 10^2 = 10^8$
g) $2^{20} \div 2^5 = 2^4$
h) $3^{12} \div 3^4 = 3^8$
i) $4^6 \div 6^4 = 4^2$
j) $10^{20} \div 10^3 = 10^{17}$
k) $4^6 \div (4^2 \times 4^3) = 4^1$
l) $9^2 \times (9^{30} \div 9^{25}) = 9^{10}$

Q6 Remove the brackets from the following and express as a single power:
a) $(3^4 \times 3^2) \div (3^6 \times 3^3)$
b) $(4^{10} \times 4^{12}) \times 4^3$
c) $10^2 \div (10^3 \times 10^{12})$
d) $(3^6)^{-2}$
e) $4^2 \times 4^{-1} \times 4^6 \times (4^2 \div 4^3)$
f) $(5^2 \times 5^3) \div (5^6 \div 5^4)$

SECTION TWO — MORE NUMBERS

Powers and Roots

Evaluate the expressions in questions 7 to 11. Give your answers to 3 s.f. where necessary.

Q7 a) $(6.5)^3$

b) $(0.35)^2$

c) $(15.2)^4$

d) $(0.04)^3$

e) $\sqrt{5.6}$

f) $\sqrt[3]{12.4}$

g) $\sqrt{109}$

h) $\sqrt[3]{0.6}$

i) $(1\frac{1}{2})^2$

j) $\sqrt{4\frac{3}{4}}$

k) $\left(\frac{5}{8}\right)^3$

l) $\sqrt[3]{\frac{9}{10}}$

Q8 a) $(2.4)^2 + 3$

b) $5.9 - (1.2)^3$

c) $\sqrt[3]{5.6} + (4.2)^2$

d) $(6.05)^3 - \sqrt[3]{8.4}$

e) $6.1[35.4 - (4.2)^2]$

f) $95 - 3(\sqrt[3]{48} - 2.6)$

g) $1\frac{1}{2}[4 + (2\frac{1}{4})^2]$

h) $19 - 4[(\frac{1}{4})^2 + ((\frac{5}{8})^3)]$

i) $15\frac{3}{5} - 2\frac{1}{2}\left[(1\frac{3}{4})^3 - \sqrt[3]{1\frac{1}{2}}\right]$

Q9 a) 5^{-3}

b) 2^{-2}

c) 16^{-4}

d) $(1.5)^{-1}$

e) $5^{\frac{1}{2}}$

f) $6^{\frac{1}{3}}$

g) $9^{\frac{1}{5}}$

h) $(4.2)^{\frac{2}{3}}$

i) $(1\frac{1}{4})^{-3}$

j) $(2\frac{3}{5})^{\frac{1}{5}}$

k) $(5\frac{1}{3})^{-2}$

l) $(10\frac{5}{6})^{\frac{5}{6}}$

Remember — fractional powers mean roots.

Q10 a) $\sqrt{(1.4)^2 + (0.5)^2}$

b) $5.9[(2.3)^{1/4} + (4.7)^{1/2}]$

c) $2.5 - 0.6[(7.1)^{-3} - (9.5)^{-4}]$

d) $(8.2)^{-2} + (1.6)^4 - (3.7)^{-3}$

e) $\dfrac{3\sqrt{8} - 2}{6}$

f) $\dfrac{15 + 3\sqrt{4.1}}{2.4}$

g) $3\sqrt{4.7} - 4\sqrt{2.1}$

h) $\dfrac{(2\frac{1}{4})^{-2} - (3\frac{1}{2})^{\frac{1}{2}}}{4.4}$

Q11 a) $(2\frac{1}{4})^3 - (1.5)^2$

b) $(3.7)^{-2} + (4\frac{1}{5})^{\frac{1}{4}}$

c) $\sqrt[3]{5\frac{1}{3}} \times (4.3)^{-1}$

d) $(7.4)^{\frac{1}{3}} \times (6\frac{1}{4})^3$

e) $\dfrac{\sqrt{22\frac{1}{2}} + (3.4)^2}{(6.9)^3 \times 3.4}$

f) $\dfrac{(15\frac{3}{5})^2 \times (2.5)^{-3}}{3 \times 4\frac{1}{4}}$

g) $5[(4.3)^2 - (2.5)^{1/2}]$

h) $\dfrac{3.5(2\frac{1}{6} - \sqrt{4.1})}{(3.5)^2 \times (3\frac{1}{2})^{-2}}$

i) $\dfrac{1\frac{1}{2} + \frac{1}{4}[(2\frac{2}{3})^2 - (1.4)^2]}{(3.9)^{-3}}$

j) $\sqrt[3]{2.73} + 5\sqrt{2}$

Standard Form

Writing very big (or very small) numbers gets a bit messy with all those zeros if you don't use standard form. But of course, the main reason for knowing about standard form is... you guessed it — it's in the Exam.

Q1 Delilah is doing some calculations for her science homework.
She needs to give her answers as ordinary numbers.
How should she write the following answers?

a) 3.56×10
b) 3.56×10^3
c) 3.56×10^{-1}
d) 3.56×10^4

e) 0.082×10^2
f) 0.082×10^{-2}
g) 0.082×10
h) 0.082×10^{-1}

i) 157×10
j) 157×10^{-3}
k) 157×10^3
l) 157×10^{-1}

Q2 Write in standard form:

a) 2.56
b) 25.6
c) 0.256
d) 25 600

e) 95.2
f) 0.0952
g) 95 200
h) 0.000952

i) 4200
j) 0.0042
k) 42
l) 420.

Q3 Write in standard form:

a) 34.7×10
b) 73.004
c) 0.005×10^3
d) 9183×10^2

e) 15 million
f) 937.1×10^4
g) 0.000075
h) 0.05×10^{-2}

i) 534×10^{-2}
j) 621.03
k) 149×10^2
l) 0.003×10^{-4} .

Q4 When scientists write about massive things such as the universe, or tiny things such as cells and particles, it's often more convenient to write numbers in standard form. Write the numbers in parts a) to e) in standard form.

a) The average diameter of a cell nucleus in a mammal is around 0.006 mm.
b) A billion = a thousand million.
c) A trillion = a thousand billion.
d) A light year is 9 460 000 000 000 km (approx).
e) Nautilus covered 69 138 miles before having to refuel.

Q5 A tissue sample is three cells thick. Each cell has a thickness of 0.000004 m. What is the thickness of the tissue sample, in mm? Give your answer in standard form.

Q6 This table gives the diameter and distance from the Sun of some planets.

Planet	Distance from Sun (km)	Diameter (km)
Earth	1.5×10^8	1.3×10^4
Venus	1.085×10^8	1.2×10^4
Mars	2.28×10^8	6.8×10^3
Mercury	5.81×10^7	4.9×10^3
Jupiter	7.8×10^8	1.4×10^5
Neptune	4.52×10^9	4.9×10^4
Saturn	1.43×10^9	1.2×10^5

From the table write down which planet is:
a) smallest in diameter
b) largest in diameter
c) nearest to the Sun
d) furthest from the Sun.

Write down which planets are:
e) nearer to the Sun than the Earth
f) bigger in diameter than the Earth.

SECTION TWO — MORE NUMBERS

Standard Form

This stuff gets a lot easier if you know how to handle your calculator — read and learn.

Standard Index Form with a Calculator

Use the **EXP** button (or **EE** button) to enter numbers in standard index form.

E.g. $1.7 \times 10^9 + 2.6 \times 10^{10}$ **[1] [.] [7] [EXP] [9] [+] [2] [.] [6] [EXP] [10] [=]**

The answer is $\boxed{2.77^{\,10}}$ which is read as 2.77×10^{10}

Q7 If $x = 4 \times 10^5$ and $y = 6 \times 10^4$ work out the value of
a) xy b) $4x$ c) $3y$.

Q8 Which is <u>greater</u>, 4.62×10^{12} or 1.04×10^{13}, and <u>by how much</u>?

Q9 Which is <u>smaller</u> 3.2×10^{-8} or 1.3×10^{-9} and by how much?

Q10 The following numbers are <u>not</u> written in standard index form. Rewrite them correctly using standard index form.

a) 42×10^6 d) 11.2×10^{-5} g) 17×10^{17}
b) 38×10^{-5} e) 843×10^3 h) 28.3×10^{-5}
c) 10×10^6 f) 42.32×10^{-4} i) 10×10^{-3}

Don't forget — when you're using a calculator, you've got to write the answer as 3.46×10^{27}, <u>not</u> as 3.46^{27}. If you do it the wrong way, it means something <u>completely</u> different.

Q11 What is <u>7 million</u> in standard index form?

Q12 The radius of the Earth is 6.38×10^3 km. What is the radius of the Earth measured in <u>cm</u>? Leave your answer in standard form.

Q13 One atomic mass unit is equivalent to 1.661×10^{-27} kg. What are <u>two</u> atomic mass units equivalent to (in standard index form)?

Q14 The length of a light year, the distance light can travel in one year, is 9.461×10^{15} m. How far can light travel in
a) 2 years?
b) 6 months?
Write your answers in <u>standard form</u>.

Q15 a) The surface area of the Earth is approximately 5.1×10^8 km^2. Write this <u>without</u> using standard form.
b) The area of the Earth covered by sea is 362 000 000 km^2. Write this in standard form.
c) What is the approximate area of the Earth covered by land? Write your answer <u>without</u> using standard form.

Rounding Numbers

With all these rounding methods, you need to identify the last digit — e.g. if you're rounding 23.41 to 1 decimal place, the last digit is 4. Then look at the next digit to the right. If it's 5 or more you round up, if it's 4 or less you round down.

Q1   Round these numbers to the required number of decimal places:

a) 62.1935 (1 d.p.)   d) 19.624328 (5 d.p.)
b) 62.1935 (2 d.p.)   e) 6.2999 (3 d.p.)
c) 62.1935 (3 d.p.)   f) π (3 d.p.)

Q2   Round these numbers to the required number of significant figures.

a) 1329.62 (3 s.f.)   d) 120 (1 s.f.)
b) 1329.62 (4 s.f.)   e) 0.024687 (1 s.f.)
c) 1329.62 (5 s.f.)   f) 0.024687 (4 s.f.)

Remember — the first significant figure is the first digit which isn't zero.

Q3 $K = 456.9873$
Write K correct to:

a) one decimal place   d) three significant figures
b) two decimal places   e) two significant figures
c) three decimal places   f) one significant figure.

Q4   Calculate the square root of 8. Write your answer to two decimal places.

Q5   Calculate, giving your answers to a sensible degree of accuracy:

a) $\dfrac{42.65 \times 0.9863}{24.6 \times 2.43}$

b) $\dfrac{13.63 + 7.22}{13.63 - 7.22}$

Rounding Numbers

Whenever a measurement is rounded off to a given unit, the _actual measurement_ can be anything up to _half a unit bigger or smaller_.

1) <u>90 m</u> to the <u>nearest metre</u> could be anything between <u>85 m and 95 m</u>. (But not <u>exactly</u> equal to 95 m, or it would be rounded up to 100 m.)

2) <u>700 people</u> to the nearest <u>10 people</u> could be anything between <u>695 people and 704 people</u>. (Because this only involves <u>whole</u> numbers.)

Q6 A bumper bag of icing sugar weighs 23.4 kg. What is this correct to the nearest kilogram?

Q7 David divides £15.20 by 3. What is the answer to the nearest penny?

Q8 The great racing driver Speedy Wheelman covered 234.65 miles during the course of one of his races. Give this distance correct to the nearest mile.

Q9 Jack's company pays his travel expenses. They round the distance he drives to the nearest mile, and then pay 20p for every mile. In one week, Jack drives 95.45 miles. How much money can Jack claim back?

Q10 A pack of three model cars costs £14.30. John wants to work out what one model car would cost. What is the answer correct to the nearest penny?

Q11 Pru measured the length of her bedroom as 2.345 metres. Give this measurement correct to the nearest centimetre.

Q12 At a golf club, a putting green is given as being 5 m long to the nearest metre. Give the range of values that the actual length of the green could be.

Q13 Carlo weighs himself on some scales that are accurate to the nearest 10 g. The digital display shows his weight as 142.46 kg.
  a) What is the maximum that he could weigh?
  b) What is the minimum that he could weigh?

Q14 a) The length of a rectangle is measured as 12 ± 0.1 cm. The width of the same rectangle is measured as 4 ± 0.1 cm. Calculate the perimeter of the rectangle, giving also the maximum possible error.

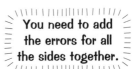
You need to add the errors for all the sides together.

  b) A rectangle measures $A ± x$ cm in length and $B ± y$ cm in width. The formula $P = 2(A + B)$ is used to calculate the perimeter, P, of the rectangle. What is the maximum possible error in P?

Accuracy

We're back to significant figures again.
Still, it's all good practice, and practice makes...

1) For fairly <u>CASUAL MEASUREMENTS, 2 SIGNIFICANT FIGURES</u> are most appropriate.

Cooking — 250 g (2 s.f.) of sugar, not 253 g (3 s.f.) or 300 g (1 s.f.).

2) For <u>IMPORTANT OR TECHNICAL THINGS, 3 SIGNIFICANT FIGURES</u> are essential.

A length that will be cut to fit — you'd measure a shelf as 25.6 cm long, not 26 cm or 25.63 cm.

3) Only for <u>REALLY SCIENTIFIC WORK</u> would you need over <u>3 SIGNIFICANT FIGURES</u>.

Only someone really keen would want to know the length of a piece of
string to the nearest tenth of a millimetre — like 34.46 cm, for example.

Q1 A field is roughly rectangular with a length of 33 m 48 cm and a width of
24 m 13 cm. Farmer Jim needs to calculate the area of the field so that he
knows how much fertiliser to buy.
Calculate the area of the field in m² to:
a) 2 d.p.
b) 3 s.f.
c) State which of parts **a)** and **b)** would be the more reasonable value to use.

Just think casual, technical or really scientific...

Q2 Decide on an appropriate degree of accuracy for the following:
a) the total dry weight, 80872 kg, of the space shuttle OV-102
Columbia with its 3 main engines
b) the distance of 3.872 miles from Mel's house to Bryan's house
c) 1.563 m of fabric required to make a bedroom curtain
d) 152.016 kg of coal delivered to Jeff's house
e) 6 buses owned by the Partridge Flight Bus Company
f) the maximum night temperature of 11.721 °C forecast for
Birmingham by a TV weather presenter.

Q3 Round each of the following to an appropriate degree of accuracy:
a) 42.798 g of sugar used to make a cake
b) a hall carpet of length 7.216 m
c) 3.429 g of $C_6H_{12}O_6$ (sugar) for a scientific experiment
d) 1.132 litres of lemonade used in a fruit punch
e) 0.541 miles from Jeremy's house to the nearest shop
f) 28.362 miles per gallon.

Bounds

Q1 Jodie weighs herself on some scales that are accurate to the nearest 10 grams.
The digital display shows her weight as 64.78 kg.
a) What is the maximum that she could weigh?
b) What is the minimum that she could weigh?

Q2 Sandra has a parcel to post. To find out how much it will cost she weighs it.
a) A set of kitchen scales, that weigh to the nearest 10 g, show that the parcel weighs 90 g.
Write down the largest weight that the parcel could be.
b) Next she weighs the parcel on a different set of kitchen scales, which are accurate to the
nearest 5 g. The packet weighs 95 g. Write down the upper and lower bounds of the
weight of the package according to these scales.
c) The post office weighs the parcel on some electronic scales to the nearest gram.
It weighs 98 g. Can all the scales be right?

Q3 Jimmy, Sarah and Douglas are comparing their best times for running the 1500 m.
Jimmy's best time is 5 minutes 30 seconds measured to the nearest 10 seconds.
Sarah's best time is also 5 minutes 30 seconds, but measured to the nearest 5 seconds.
Douglas' best time is 5 minutes 26 seconds measured to the nearest second.

a) What are the upper and lower bounds for Sarah's best time?
b) Of the three Douglas thinks that he is the quickest at running the 1500 m.
Explain why this may not be the case.

Q4 A rug is 1.8 m long and 0.7 m wide. Both measurements are given correct to 1 d.p.
a) State the minimum possible length of the rug.
b) Calculate the maximum possible area of the rug.

Q5 $R = \dfrac{S}{T}$ is a formula used by stockbrokers.
$S = 940$, correct to 2 significant figures and $T = 5.56$, correct to 3 significant figures.
a) For the value of S, write down the upper bound and the lower bound.
b) For the value of T, write down the upper bound and the lower bound.
c) Calculate the upper bound and lower bound for R.
d) Write down the value of R correct to an appropriate number of significant figures.

Q6 $A = 13$, correct to 2 significant figures. $B = 12.5$, correct to 3 significant figures.
a) For the value of A, write down the upper bound and the lower bound.
b) For the value of B, write down the upper bound and the lower bound.
c) Calculate the upper bound and lower bound for C when $C = AB$.

Q7 Vince ran a 100 m race in 10.3 seconds. If the time was measured to the nearest
0.1 seconds and the distance to the nearest metre, what is the maximum value of his
average speed, in metres per second?

Q8 A lorry travelled 125 kilometres in 1 hour and 50 minutes. If the time was measured
to the nearest 10 minutes and the distance to the nearest five kilometres, what was the
maximum value of the average speed of the lorry, in kilometres per hour?

Estimating

Q1 Without using your calculator find approximate answers to the following:

a) 6560 × 1.97
b) 8091 × 1.456
c) 38.45 × 1.4237 × 5.0002
d) 45.34 ÷ 9.345
e) 34504 ÷ 7133
f) $\dfrac{55.33 \times 19.345}{9.23}$

g) 7139 × 2.13
h) 98 × 2.54 × 2.033
i) 21 × 21 × 21
j) 8143 ÷ 81
k) 62000 ÷ 950
l) π ÷ 3

Turn these into nice easy numbers that you can deal with without a calculator.

Q2 At the start of the week, a shop had approximately 15 000 cartons of broccoli juice in stock. The shop sold 1483 cartons on Monday, 2649 on Tuesday, 1539 on Wednesday, 1478 on Thursday and 2958 on Friday. Estimate the number of cartons remaining.

Q3 Estimate the area under the graph.

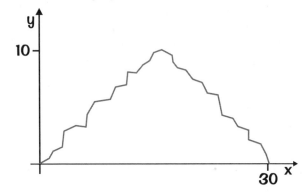

Q4 A supermarket chain sold 14634 tins of beans during a four week period.
a) If the supermarkets were open every day of the week, how many days did it take to sell the 14634 tins of beans?
b) What was the average number of tins of beans sold each day?
c) Show your working for a rough estimate to b) to check that your answer is of the right order of magnitude.

"of the right order of magnitude" is just a posh way to say "the right size", by the way.

Q5 π is the number of times that the diameter of a circle divides into the circumference. Many values have been used as estimates — here are a few examples:

$$3, \ \frac{22}{7}, \ \sqrt{10}, \ \frac{255}{81}, \ 3\frac{17}{120}.$$

a) Use your calculator to give each estimate correct to 7 decimal places.
b) Which is the most accurate estimate for π?

Q6 Showing all your working, estimate the value of the following:

a) $\dfrac{144.5 + 49.1}{153.2 - 41.2}$

b) $\dfrac{18.2 \times 10.7}{\sqrt{398.6}}$

c) $\dfrac{2021.23 \times 4.0436}{20.33 \times 4.902}$

d) $\dfrac{(9.2)^2 \div 10.3}{4.306 \times 5.011}$

SECTION TWO — MORE NUMBERS

Estimating

Q7 Estimate the areas of the following:

a)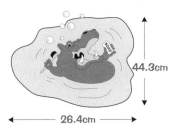

44.3cm

26.4cm

b)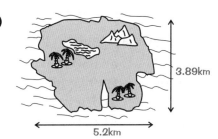

3.89km

5.2km

Q8 Joan needs to estimate the size of her bedroom so that she can buy enough paint to cover the walls. Two of the walls measure 2.86 m by 3.16 m, and the other two walls measure 2.86 m by 3.42 m.
a) Estimate the area that Joan needs to paint in m².
b) If one tin of paint will cover 15 m², how many tins of paint will Joan need to paint her bedroom?

Q9 Estimate these volumes:

a)

4cm

9.7cm

3.1cm

b)

10cm

22.3cm

Q10 Mark wants to buy some tropical fish.
The pet shop owner tells him that he will need a tank with a volume of at least 7000 cm³.
Estimate whether Mark's tank will be big enough.

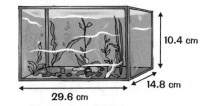

10.4 cm

14.8 cm

29.6 cm

Q11 Here is a sequence of square numbers. Use it to estimate (to 1 d.p.) the square roots below.

12	13	14	15	16	17	18	19	20
144	169	196	225	256	289	324	361	400

a) $\sqrt{405}$ **b)** $\sqrt{270}$ **c)** $\sqrt{250}$ **d)** $\sqrt{375}$ **e)** $\sqrt{391}$

Q12 Estimate the following square roots, to 1 d.p.:

a) $\sqrt{48}$ **c)** $\sqrt{84}$ **e)** $\sqrt{98}$
b) $\sqrt{118}$ **d)** $\sqrt{17}$ **f)** $\sqrt{34}$

Start with square roots that you know — and use them to make an educated <u>guess</u>.

Q13 Now estimate these (they're a bit harder) — again, to 1 d.p.:

a) $\sqrt{41}$ **c)** $\sqrt{30}$ **e)** $\sqrt{180}$

b) $\sqrt{200}$ **d)** $\sqrt{150}$ **f)** $\sqrt{140}$

Conversion Factors

You've got to know all the metric and imperial conversion factors — there's no way out of it, you'll just have to sit down and learn them, sorry and all that...

Q1 Express the given quantity in the unit(s) in brackets:

a) 2 m [cm]
b) 3.3 cm [mm]
c) 4 kg [g]
d) 600 g [kg]

e) 650 m [km]
f) 9 kg [g]
g) 7 g [kg]
h) 950 g [kg]

i) 6 m [mm]
j) 2 tonnes [kg]
k) 3000 g [kg]
l) 8 cm 6 mm [mm]

m) 550 kg [tonnes]
n) 3 m 54 cm [cm]
o) 0.7 cm [mm]
p) 4200 ml [l]

Q2 A seamstress needs to cut a 47 cm strip of finest Chinese silk.
a) How many m is this?
b) How many mm is this?

Q3 The priceless Greek statue in my garden is 3 metres tall.

a) How many cm is this?
b) How many mm is this?
c) How many km is this?

Q4 The scale on a map is 1:10 000. How big are the following in real life? Give your answers in km.
a) a distance of 2 cm on the map
b) a distance of 20 cm on the map
c) a distance of 70 cm on the map
d) an area of 2 cm² on the map?

Maps can be tricky. Best thing is to keep the units the same when you do the initial conversion, then do another conversion to the appropriate units.

Q5 Another map has a scale of 1:3000. What size on this map are the following? Give your answers in cm.
a) a distance of 5 km in real life
b) a distance of 1 km in real life
c) an area of 100 m² in real life
d) an area of 50 m² in real life?

Just remember — the distance on the map is unlikely to be larger than the real-life distance.

Q6 Justin is shopping online. He looks up the following exchange rates:

1.60 US dollars ($) to £1 sterling.

150 Japanese yen (¥) to £1 sterling.

Calculate to the nearest penny the cost in pounds sterling of each of Justin's purchases:
a) A book costing $7.50
b) An MP3 player costing ¥7660

Time

Q1   The times below are given using a 24-hour system.
Using am or pm, give the equivalent time for a 12-hour clock.

a) 0500   **c)** 0316   **e)** 2230
b) 1448   **d)** 1558   **f)** 0001

Q2   The times below are taken from a 12-hour clock. Give the equivalent 24-hour readings.

a) 11.30 pm   **c)** 12.15 am   **e)** 8.30 am
b) 10.22 am   **d)** 12.15 pm   **f)** 4.45 pm

Q3   Joe is watching a film. It starts at 19.55 and ends at 22.20.
How many minutes does the film last?

Q4   Find the time elapsed between the following pairs of times:

a) 0820 on 1 October 2010 and 1620 on the same day
b) 10.22 pm on 1 October 2010 and 8.22 am the next day
c) 2.18 am on 1 October 2010 and 2.14 pm later the same day
d) 0310 on 1 October 2010 and 0258 on 3 October 2010.

Q5   Convert the following into hours and minutes:

a) 3.25 hours   **b)** 0.4 hours   **c)** 7.3 hours   **d)** 1.2 hours.

Q6   Convert the following into just hours:

a) 2 hours and 20 minutes
b) 3 hours and 6 minutes
c) 20 minutes.

Q7   This timetable refers to three trains that travel from Asham to Derton.
a) Which train is quickest from Asham to Derton?
b) Which train is quickest from Cottingham to Derton?

Asham – Derton			
	Train 1	Train 2	Train 3
Asham	0832	1135	1336
Bordhouse	0914	1216	1414
Cottingham	1002	1259	1456
Derton	1101	1404	1602

c) I live in Bordhouse. It takes me 8 minutes to walk to the train station.
At what time must I leave the house by to arrive in Derton before 2.30 pm?

Speed, Distance and Time

This is an easy enough formula — and of course you can put it in that good old formula triangle as well.

Average speed = $\dfrac{\text{Total distance}}{\text{Total time}}$

Q1   A train travels 240 km in 4 hours. What is its <u>average speed</u>?

Q2   A car travels for 3 hours at an average speed of 55 km/h. How far has it travelled?

Q3   A boy rides a bike at an average speed of 15 km/h. How long will it take him to ride 40 km?

Q4   <u>Complete</u> this table.

Distance Travelled	Time Taken	Average Speed
210 km	3 hrs	
135 km		30 km/h
	2 hrs 30 mins	42 km/h
9 km	45 mins	
640 km		800 km/h
	1 hr 10 mins	60 km/h

Q5   An athlete can run 100 m in 11 seconds.
Calculate the athlete's speed in:
a) m/s
b) km/h.

Q6   A plane flies over city A at 09.55 and over city B at 10.02.
What is its <u>average</u> speed if these cities are 63 km apart? Give your answer in km/h.

Q7   The distance from Kendal (Oxenholme) to London (Euston) is 420 km. The train travels at an average speed of 115 km/h. Pete needs to be in London by 10.30. If he catches the 07.05 from Kendal, will he be in London on time? <u>Show all your working</u>.

Q8   In a speed trial a sand yacht travelled a measured kilometre in 36.4 seconds.
a) Calculate this speed in km/h.
   On the return kilometre it took 36.16 seconds.
b) Find the <u>total time</u> for the two runs.
c) Calculate the average speed of the two runs in km/h.

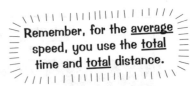

Remember, for the <u>average</u> speed, you use the <u>total</u> time and <u>total</u> distance.

Q9   A motorist drives from Manchester to London. 290 km is on motorway where he averages 100 km/h. 90 km is on city roads where he averages 45 km/h, and 25 km is on country roads where he averages 40 km/h.
a) Calculate the total time taken for the journey.
b) How far did he travel altogether?
c) Calculate the average speed for the journey.

Speed, Distance and Time

Q10 Victor walks at an average speed of 4 km/h. He needs to walk to Askam-in-Furness, 3 km away. He needs to be there at 3.00 pm. What time should he set off?

Q11 The distance between two railway stations is 145 km.
  a) How long does a train travelling at 65 km/h on average take to travel this distance?
  b) Another train travels on a parallel track at an average speed of 80 km/h but has a 10 min stop during the journey. How long does this second train take?
  c) If both arrive at 1600, what time did each leave?

Q12 Two athletes ran a road race. One ran at an average speed of 16 km/h, the other at 4 m/s. Which was the fastest? How long would each take to run 10 km?

Q13 A plane leaves Amsterdam at 0715 and flies at an average speed of 650 km/h to Paris, arriving at 0800. It takes off again at 0840 and flies at the same average speed to Nice arriving at 1005.
  a) How far is it from Amsterdam to Paris?
  b) How far is it from Paris to Nice?
  c) What was the average speed for the whole journey?

Q14 A runner covered the first 100 m of a 200 m race in 12.3 seconds.
  a) What was his average speed for the first 100 m?
  b) The second 100 m took 15.1 seconds. What was his average speed for the 200 m?

Q15 A military plane can achieve a speed of 1100 km/h. At this speed it passes over town A at 1205 and town B at 1217.
  a) How far apart are towns A and B?
  b) The plane then flies over village C, which is 93 km from B. How long does it take from B to C?

Q16 Two cars set off on 290 km journeys. One travels mostly on A roads and manages an average speed of 68 km/h. The other car travels mostly on the motorway and achieves an average speed of 103 km/h when the car is moving, but the driver stops for a break. If they both take the same time over the journey, for how long does the second car stop?

Q17 A stone is dropped from a cliff top. After 1 second it has fallen 4.8 m, after 2 seconds a total of 19.2 m and after 3 seconds 43.2 m. Calculate its average speed:
  a) in the first second
  b) in the second second
  c) for all 3 seconds
  d) Change all the m/s speeds to km/h.

Q18 In 1990 three motor racers had fastest lap speeds of 236.6, 233.8 and 227.3 km/h. If 1 km = 0.62 miles, how long would each driver take to lap 5 miles at these speeds?

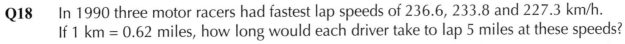

SECTION TWO — MORE NUMBERS

Order of Operations

Nothing weird here. Just a load of sums to do — while you're at it remember BODMAS.
Both Ocelots Demand Myriad Antique Similes. Hang on, that's not right...
Brackets, Other, Division, Multiplication, Addition, Subtraction. That's better.

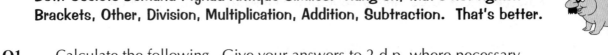

Q1 Calculate the following. Give your answers to 2 d.p. where necessary.

a) $6 + 4 \div 2$

b) $(6 + 4) \div 2$

c) $(2 \times 6) - (7 \div 3)^2$

d) $2 \times 6 - 7 \div 3^2$

e) $8 \div (9 \times 3^2) - 1$

f) $4 \times 4^2 + (4 \times 4)^2 - (4 \div 4)^3 \div 4^3$

g) $7 \div (6 \div 3) + 2$

h) $10^3 - (-5)^2 + (64 \div 8)$

i) $(3 \times 3) + 24 \div (2 - 14)^2$

j) $11 \times (77 \div 7) + 121 - 2 \times (10 + 1)^2$

Q2 Calculate the following. Give your answers to 2 d.p. where necessary.

a) $10 + \sqrt{16} - (42 \div 7)$

b) $\sqrt{36} \div 2 + (5 \times 14)$

c) $91 + (\sqrt{289} \times 2) - 12$

d) $\sqrt{1} \times 42 \div 6$

e) $2 + (\sqrt{81} + 3)^2 \div 7$

f) $(\sqrt{400} - 18)^3 + (4 \div 6)$

g) $\sqrt{9} \div 3 \times 2 - 1$

h) $\sqrt{7} + \sqrt{5} - (\sqrt{3} \times 2)$

i) $\sqrt{626} - (4 + 56 \div 3)^2$

j) $(12 - \sqrt{4912}) \div 15^2$

Q3 Calculate the following. Give your answers to 2 d.p. where necessary.

a) $\dfrac{21}{2 + 5}$

b) $\dfrac{3^2}{9 + 9^2}$

c) $\dfrac{\sqrt{16}}{3 \div 12}$

d) $\dfrac{5^2}{\sqrt{49} - 4}$

e) $\dfrac{1 - \sqrt{17}}{\sqrt{45} + 22^2}$

f) $\dfrac{18^2}{2 + \sqrt[3]{17}}$

g) $\dfrac{15^2 - 2^3}{\sqrt{12} - \sqrt{22}}$

h) $\dfrac{4 \times \sqrt[3]{3}}{24 + \sqrt[3]{30}}$

i) $\dfrac{14 + (3 \div 7)}{(3^3 - \sqrt{5})}$

j) $\dfrac{\sqrt[3]{177} - \sqrt{2}}{\sqrt{15} \times 4}$

k) $\dfrac{\sqrt{(81 \div 4)}}{7^3 - (31 \times 0.3)}$

l) $\sqrt{\dfrac{7}{4^3}} - (53 \div 2^4)^2$

Calculator Buttons

Q1 Using the x^2 button on your calculator, work out:

a) 1^2 d) 16^2 g) $(-5)^2$

b) 2^2 e) $(-1)^2$ h) 1000^2

c) 11^2 f) 30^2 i) 0^2

Q2 Using the $\sqrt{}$ button on your calculator, work out:

a) $\sqrt{16}$ d) $\sqrt{0}$ g) $\sqrt{3}$

b) $\sqrt{36}$ e) $\sqrt{3600}$ h) $\sqrt{7}$

c) $\sqrt{289}$ f) $\sqrt{400}$ i) $\sqrt{30}$

Q3 Use the $\sqrt[3]{}$ button on your calculator to work out:

a) $\sqrt[3]{1}$ e) $\sqrt[3]{27}$

b) $\sqrt[3]{0}$ f) $\sqrt[3]{-27}$

c) $\sqrt[3]{343}$ g) $\sqrt[3]{-64}$

d) $\sqrt[3]{1000}$ h) $\sqrt[3]{-5}$

Yeah, OK, we all know how to do sums on a calculator — but it can do so much more... check out the groovy powers button and the funky brackets buttons, not to mention the slinky $1/x$ button...

Q4 By calculating the bottom line (the denominator) first and storing it in your calculator, work out:

a) $\dfrac{21}{2 + \sin 30°}$ c) $\dfrac{15}{\cos 30° + 22}$ e) $\dfrac{12}{12 + \tan 60°}$

b) $\dfrac{\tan 15°}{12 + 12^2}$ d) $\dfrac{18}{3 + \sqrt[3]{12}}$ f) $\dfrac{18}{11 + \tan 77°}$

Q5 Using the $a\frac{b}{c}$ button on your calculator:

a) reduce to the lowest terms: i) $\dfrac{3}{9}$ ii) $\dfrac{56}{91}$ iii) $\dfrac{512}{4096}$

b) convert to mixed fractions: i) $\dfrac{17}{5}$ ii) $\dfrac{223}{24}$ iii) $\dfrac{9658}{214}$

c) convert to top-heavy fractions: i) $2\frac{1}{3}$ ii) $8\frac{11}{23}$ iii) $41\frac{52}{63}$

Calculator Buttons

Q6   Using [(--- and ---)] , calculate:

Here comes BODMAS...

a) $\dfrac{(14+18)}{(2\times 8)}$

c) $\dfrac{(9+(4\div 2))}{(11\times 3)}$

e) $\dfrac{12}{(8+9)(13-11)}$

b) $\dfrac{8}{(1\times 4)(8-6)}$

d) $\dfrac{14(4\times 8)}{(6+9)}$

f) $\dfrac{7(5+4)}{12(9\times 8)}$

Q7   Using the x^y or $\wedge$ button, find:

a) 2^0

b) 4^{10}

c) 2^{20}

d) π^2

e) 2^{-1}

f) 3^{10}

g) $(\cos 30°)^5$

h) 4.29^7

i) $(\sin 45°)^4$

For entering numbers into your calculator in standard form you need the **EXP** or **EE** button. It actually means $\times 10^n$ so be careful not to type in the $\times 10$ part.

E.g. to enter 3.4×10^5 you would only need to type [3] [•] [4] [EXP] [5] [=] and **not** [3] [•] [4] [×] [10] [EXP] [5] [=]

Q8   Enter the following numbers into your calculator and write down what you get:

a) 4×10^3

b) 1×10^4

c) 6.2×10^5

Q9   Work out:

a) $\dfrac{2\times 10^2}{5\times 10^1}$

d) $\dfrac{2.3\times 10^5}{4.6\times 10^6}$

b) $\dfrac{4.2\times 10^4}{2.1\times 10^5}$

e) $\dfrac{7.0\times 10^3}{3.5\times 10^5}$

c) $\dfrac{1.92\times 10^3}{9.6\times 10^2}$

f) $\dfrac{4.44\times 10^4}{1.11\times 10^2}$

Sets

Sets aren't scary — they're just collections of things. The tricky bit is showing how these things relate to each other. There are diagrams to draw and symbols to learn. Here are some questions to practise with...

Q1 The elements of set E are all the prime numbers less than 12.
  a) Write set E as a rule using set notation.
  b) Write set E as a complete list of its elements.

Q2 H = {1, 4, 9, 16, 20, 36, 49, 64, 81, 100}
  K = {Integers}
  L = {Natural numbers ≤ 0}
  a) Which one of these sets = ∅   L
  b) Write down a number that is an element of set K and one that is not an element of set K using set notation.

  $K = \{ 4 \}$
  $K' = \{ 5 \}$

Q3 Set B is shown in the Venn diagram below:

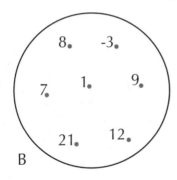

8.   -3.
7.   1.   9.
21.   12.

B

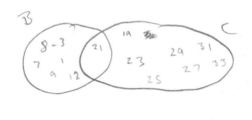

  a) Write set B as a complete list of its elements.
  b) Draw a Venn diagram for set C = {odd numbers between 18 and 34}.

Q4 Draw a Venn diagram for:
  a) A = {odd numbers less than 20} and B = {prime numbers less than 20}
  b) C = {integers greater than or equal to -4 and less than or equal to 4} and
  D = {natural numbers less than 5}

Q5 Using the Venn diagram on the right find:
  a) Set R as a list of its elements
  b) n(S) 9
  c) Set R ∩ S   1, 64
  d) n(R ∪ S) 11

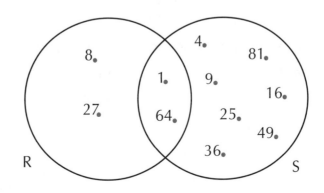

8.   4.   81.
1.   9.
27.   16.
64.   25.
49.
36.

R   S

Sets

Q6 This Venn diagram shows the results of a survey about revision. Set D shows those people who listen to dolphins and set P those who take advice from peacocks.

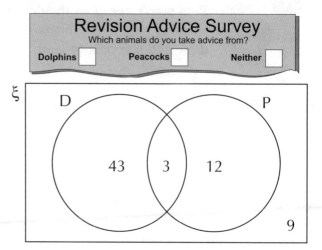

a) What does the universal set, ξ, represent in this diagram?

b) How many people don't take revision advice from dolphins or peacocks? 9

c) Find $n(D \cup P)$ and $n(D \cap P)$.

    58   3

Q7 John travels around Milton Keynes and counts different types of cows. In addition to real cows he finds artificial cows made from three different materials and some made from a combination of those materials. He records his findings in sets — Concrete (C), Glass (G) and Plastic (P).

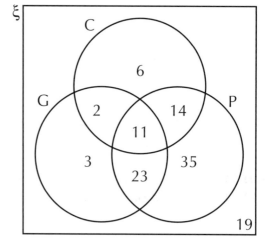

a) What is John's universal set?

b) How many real cows did he find? 19

c) Find $n(P)$. 83

d) Find $n(C \cup G)$. 59

e) Find $n(C')$. 80

f) Find $n(C \cap P)$. 25

g) Find $n(C \cap G \cap P)$. 11

h) How many cows are made from glass and plastic but not concrete? 23 Write this is set notation.

    $n(G \cap P \cap C')$

Q8 $A = \{x: 0 \le x \le 18\}$
$B = \{y: y \text{ is a multiple of 3}\}$
$C = \{z: z \text{ is a factor of 15}\}$

Say whether the following statements about sets A, B and C are true or false.

a) $0 \notin A$ false

b) $0 \in C$ false

c) $\frac{2}{3} \in A$ false

d) $B \subset A$

e) $A \subset C$

f) $C \subset B$

g) $C \subset A$

h) $\{6\} \in B$

i) $\{6\} \subset B$

j) $6 \subset B$

k) $(B \cap C) \subset A$

l) $(B \cup C) \subset A$

Formulas from Words

It's no big mystery — algebra is just like normal sums, but with the odd letter or two stuck in for good measure.

Q1 Write an algebraic expression for each of these:

a) To find y add 5 to x

b) To find y multiply x by 7 and add 4

c) To find y subtract 7 from x and divide by 3

d) To find y square 6 and add it to x

e) Square x then divide by 8 to find y

f) y is equal to the square of x divided by 12

Q2 Tickets for a football match cost £25 each.

a) Write a formula to calculate the cost, c, of n tickets.

b) A booking fee of £1.25 is added to each ticket bought online. Write an equation to calculate the cost of n tickets bought online.

CGP Wanderers Football Club
Vs United Rovers FC
Comfy Seat
East stand lower bit
Row 20
Seat 104
£25.00

Q3 There are n books in a pile. Write an expression for the number (N) of books in:

a) A pile with 23 more books

b) A pile with 14 fewer books

c) A pile with twice as many books

d) x piles each with n books in them

e) A warehouse filled with a square of book piles x piles long each side.

Q4 a) This square has sides of length d cm.

i) What is its perimeter?

ii) What is its area?

b) For the triangle below write equations for:

i) Its perimeter

ii) Its area.

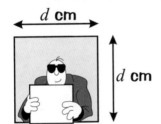

d cm

d cm

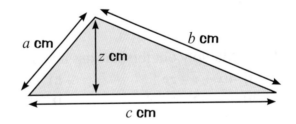

a cm

b cm

z cm

c cm

Q5 The cost (C) of hiring a mountain bike is £10, plus £5 for each hour you use the bike (h). Write down a formula that can be used for working out the cost of hiring a bike.

Q6 The cost per person of a flight from Manchester to Aberdeen is £73 plus £27 tax and an extra £15 for each piece of luggage. Write down a formula to calculate the total cost (T) of a flight for p people with a total of l pieces of luggage.

Q7 The number of sheep (S) that a dragon can eat per day is 3 plus a third of its wingspan in metres (w). Write an expression to calculate how many sheep a dragon can eat in d days.

Basic Algebra

Q1 Work out the following temperature changes:
a) 20 °C to -7 °C
b) -10 °C to -32 °C
c) -17 °C to -5 °C
d) -3 °C to 15 °C
e) -31 °C to -16 °C
f) -5 °C to -17 °C

Q2 Which is larger and by how much?
a) $-12 + 7 - 4 + 6 - 2 + 7$ or b) $-30 + 26 - 3 - 7 + 17$

Q3 Simplify: a) $4x - 5x + 3x - x + 2x - 7x$ b) $30y - 10y + 2y - 3y + 4y - 5y$

Q4 Find the value of xy and $\frac{x}{y}$ for each of the following:
a) $x = -100$ $y = 10$
b) $x = 24$ $y = -4$
c) $x = -48$ $y = -3$
d) $x = 0$ $y = -4$

Q5 Find the value of $(a - b) \div (c + d)$ when $a = 10$, $b = -26$, $c = -5$ and $d = -4$.

Q6 Simplify the following:
a) $2x \times -3y$
b) $-8a \times 2b$
c) $-4x \times -2x$
d) $4p \times -4p$
e) $-30x \div -3y$
f) $50x \div -5y$
g) $10x \div -2y$
h) $-30x \div -10x$
i) $40ab \div -10ab$
j) $70x^2 \div -7x^2$
k) $-36x^2 \div -9x$
l) $40y^2 \div -5y$

Q7 Simplify the following by collecting like terms together:
a) $3x^2 + 4x + 12x^2 - 5x$
b) $14x^2 - 10x - x^2 + 5x$
c) $12 - 4x^2 + 10x - 3x^2 + 2x$
d) $20abc + 12ab + 10bac + 4b$
e) $8pq + 7p + q + 10qp - q + p$
f) $15ab - 10a + b - 7a + 2ba$
g) $4pq - 14p - 8q + p - q + 8p$
h) $13x^2 + 4x^2 - 5y^2 + y^2 - x^2$
i) $11ab + 2cd - ba - 13dc + abc$
j) $3x^2 + 4xy + 2y^2 - z^2 + 2xy - y^2 - 5x^2$

Q8 Multiply out the brackets and simplify where possible:
a) $4(x + y - z)$
b) $x(x + 5)$
c) $-3(x - 2)$
d) $7(a + b) + 2(a + b)$
e) $3(a + 2b) - 2(2a + b)$
f) $4(x - 2) - 2(x - 1)$
g) $4e(e + 2f) + 2f(e - f)$
h) $14(2m - n) + 2(3n - 6m)$
i) $4x(x + 2) - 2x(3 - x)$
j) $3(2 + ab) + 5(1 - ab)$
k) $(x - 2y)z - 2x(x + z)$
l) $4(x - 2y) - (5 + x - 2y)$
m) $a - 4(a + b)$
n) $4pq(2 + r) + 5qr(2p + 7)$
o) $x^2(x + 1)$
p) $4x^2\left(x + 2 + \dfrac{1}{x}\right)$
q) $8ab(a + 3 + b)$
r) $7pq\left(p + q - \dfrac{1}{p}\right)$
s) $4[(x + y) - 3(y - x)]$

Q9 For each of the large rectangles below, write down the area of each of the small rectangles and hence find an expression for the area of the large rectangle.

a)

b)

c)
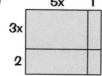

Eeeek — loads of questions...

Basic Algebra

Q10 Multiply out the brackets and simplify your answers where possible:
- **a)** $(x - 3)(x + 1)$
- **b)** $(x - 3)(x + 5)$
- **c)** $(x + 10)(x + 3)$
- **d)** $(x - 5)(x - 2)$
- **e)** $(x + 2)(x - 7)$
- **f)** $(4 - x)(7 - x)$

Q11 A rectangular pond has length $(5 - x)$ m and width $(x - 2)$ m.
Write down a simplified expression for:
- **a)** the pond's perimeter
- **b)** the pond's area.

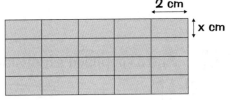

Q12 A rectangular bar of chocolate consists of 20 small rectangular pieces. The size of a small rectangular piece of chocolate is 2 cm by x cm.

- **a)** Write down an expression for the perimeter of the whole bar.
- **b)** Write down an expression for the area of the whole bar.
- **c)** If I ate 6 small rectangular pieces of chocolate, what is the area of the remaining bar?

Q13 Find a simplified expression for the perimeter *and* the area of the following shapes.

- **a)**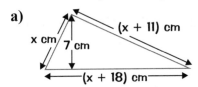
- **b)**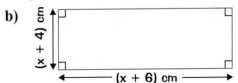

Q14 All the expressions below have a as a common factor. Factorise each of them.
- **a)** $a^2b + ac$
- **b)** $5a + 13a^2b$
- **c)** $2a^2b + 3ac$
- **d)** $a^3 + ay$
- **e)** $2ax + 3a^2y + 4a^2z$
- **f)** $ab^2 + a^3c^2$

Q15 Write the following out in full. E.g. $c^3 = c \times c \times c$
- **a)** k^2
- **b)** p^3q^2
- **c)** gt^2
- **d)** $(gt)^2$
- **e)** $(-t)^2$
- **f)** $-(t)^2$

Q16 Write the following in index notation:
- **a)** $a \times a \times a$
- **b)** $c \times c \times c \times c \times c$
- **c)** $a \times a \times b \times b \times b$
- **d)** $d \times c \times c \times d \times c$
- **e)** $x \times 2x \times 2x$
- **f)** $-y \times 3x \times 2y \times -y$

Q17 Use index laws to simplify the following where possible:
- **a)** $x^3 \times x^2$
- **b)** $x^3 \div x^2$
- **c)** $-(y)^5 \times y^8$
- **d)** $q^{11} \div q^8$
- **e)** $(b^5)(b^4)$
- **f)** $x^3 + x^2$
- **g)** $-(f)^8 \div f$
- **h)** $x^3y^6 \times x^4y$
- **i)** $p^9q^2 \times q^4$
- **j)** $(-x)^2 \div -x$
- **k)** $y^7 \div y^7$
- **l)** k^0
- **m)** $u^3 \times u^0$
- **n)** 1^x
- **o)** $(gt)^1$
- **p)** $r^3 \div r^3$
- **q)** $(k^2)^5$
- **r)** $(p^3)^2$
- **s)** $\dfrac{v^4}{v^2}$
- **t)** $\dfrac{i^6}{i^5}$
- **u)** $(gt^2)^7$
- **v)** $(x^3)^3 \times x^2$
- **w)** $\dfrac{r^4 \times r^4}{r^3 \times r^2}$

Basic Algebra

Q18 Multiply out the brackets and simplify your answers where possible:
- **a)** $(2 + 3x)(3x - 1)$
- **b)** $(3x + 2)(2x - 4)$
- **c)** $(x - 3)(4x + 1)$
- **d)** $2(2x + y)(x - 2y)$
- **e)** $4(x + 2y)(3x - 2y)$
- **f)** $(3x + 2y)^2$

Q19 Find the product of $5x - 2$ and $3x + 2$.

Q20 Find the square of $2x - 1$.

Q21 Find a simplified expression for the perimeter *and* the area of the following shapes.

a)

(4x – 1) cm

b)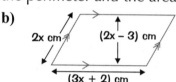

Q22 Factorise and simplify the following:
- **a)** $4xy^2z + 8xyz^2$
- **b)** $8x^2yz^2 + 12xy^2z$
- **c)** $8xyz + 16x^2yz$
- **d)** $20x^2y^2z^2 + 16xyz^2$

Q23 Rewrite the following **without** using negative powers:
- **a)** k^{-2}
- **b)** $p^{-3}q^2$
- **c)** gt^{-2}
- **d)** $\dfrac{1}{y^{-2}}$
- **e)** $\dfrac{a^4}{v^{-2}}$
- **f)** $\dfrac{v^{-2}a^4}{b}$

Q24 Simplify the following and write your answer **without** using negative powers:
- **a)** $h^2 \times h^{-8}$
- **b)** $g \div g^4$
- **c)** $(t^2)^4 \times (t^3)^{-4}$
- **d)** $\dfrac{v^{-4}}{v^{-2}}$
- **e)** $\dfrac{w^4}{w^5}$
- **f)** $\dfrac{a^4 \times a^2}{(a^5)^2}$

Q25 These expressions all involve fractional powers. Simplify them as far as possible.
- **a)** $(9a^6)^{\frac{1}{2}}$
- **b)** $(p^8q^{10})^{\frac{1}{2}}$
- **c)** $(x^9y^{12})^{\frac{1}{3}}$
- **d)** $(x^3)^{\frac{2}{3}}$
- **e)** $(64x^3)^{\frac{1}{6}}$
- **f)** $(36j^4)^{-\frac{1}{2}}$
- **g)** $\dfrac{4b^{\frac{1}{2}} \times b^{\frac{2}{5}}}{32b^{\frac{1}{5}}}$
- **h)** $(81u)^{\frac{1}{4}} \times u^{-\frac{3}{4}}$
- **i)** $\dfrac{(100d)^{\frac{1}{2}} \div d^{\frac{1}{4}}}{d^{\frac{1}{8}}}$

Algebraic Fractions

Q1   Simplify the following by cancelling down where possible:

a) $\dfrac{27x^4y^2z}{9x^3yz^2}$ **b)** $\dfrac{48a^2b^2}{(2a)^2c}$ **c)** $\dfrac{3xyz}{9x^2y^3z^4}$ **d)** $\dfrac{4p^3q^3}{(2pr)^3}$

Q2   Factorise then simplify:

a) $\dfrac{2x+4y}{x^2+2xy}$ **b)** $\dfrac{p^2-2p}{8p-16}$ **c)** $\dfrac{9vw-3v^2}{3vw-v^2}$ **d)** $\dfrac{6at^2+2at}{3at+a}$

Q3   Factorise then simplify:

a) $\dfrac{2xy^2+4x^2y}{3x^2y+6x^3}$ **b)** $\dfrac{3p^2q^2+9pq^2}{8pq+24q}$ **c)** $\dfrac{9v^2w-9v^3w}{3v^2w-3v^3}$ **d)** $\dfrac{6a^2b^2+7ab}{12ab+14}$

Q4   Multiply out the following, leaving your answers as simplified as possible:

a) $\dfrac{x^2}{y}\times\dfrac{2}{x^3}$ **e)** $\dfrac{10z^3}{xy}\times\dfrac{4x^3}{5z}$ **i)** $\dfrac{5a^2}{b}\times\dfrac{3a^2c^3}{10bd}$

b) $\dfrac{3a^4}{2}\times\dfrac{b}{a^2}$ **f)** $\dfrac{30a^2b^2c^2}{7}\times\dfrac{21c^2}{ab^3}$ **j)** $\dfrac{p^2}{pq^2}\times\dfrac{q^2}{p}$

It helps if you can cancel some factors before multiplying.

c) $\dfrac{2x}{y^2}\times\dfrac{y^3}{4x^3}$ **g)** $\dfrac{4}{x}\times\dfrac{x^3}{2}\times\dfrac{x}{10}$ **k)** $\dfrac{90r}{14t}\times\dfrac{7t^3}{30r}$

d) $\dfrac{3pq}{2}\times\dfrac{4r^2}{9p}$ **h)** $\dfrac{2a^2}{3}\times\dfrac{9b}{a}\times\dfrac{2a^2b}{5}$ **l)** $\dfrac{400d^4}{51e^5}\times\dfrac{102d^2e^4}{800e^2f}$

Q5   Divide the following, leaving your answer as simplified as possible:

a) $\dfrac{4x^3}{y}\div\dfrac{2x}{y^2}$ **e)** $\dfrac{e^2f^2}{5}\div\dfrac{ef}{10}$ **i)** $\dfrac{25a^3}{b^3}\div\dfrac{5}{b^2}$

b) $\dfrac{ab}{c}\div\dfrac{b}{c}$ **f)** $\dfrac{5x^3}{y}\div\dfrac{1}{y}$ **j)** $\dfrac{4x}{y^4z^4}\div\dfrac{2}{y^2z^3}$

c) $\dfrac{30x^3}{y^2}\div\dfrac{10x}{y}$ **g)** $\dfrac{16xyz}{3}\div\dfrac{4x^2}{9}$ **k)** $\dfrac{3m}{2n^2}\div\dfrac{m}{4n}$

d) $\dfrac{pq}{r}\div\dfrac{2}{r}$ **h)** $\dfrac{20a^3}{b^3}\div\dfrac{5}{b^2}$ **l)** $\dfrac{70f^3}{g}\div\dfrac{10f^4}{g^2}$

Q6   Solve the following equations for x:

a) $\dfrac{20x^4y^2z^3}{7xy^5}\times\dfrac{14y^3}{40x^2z^3}=5$ **b)** $\dfrac{48x^5y^2}{12z^3}\div\dfrac{16x^2y^2}{z^3}=2$

Algebraic Fractions

OK, I guess it gets a bit tricky here — you've got to cross-multiply to get a common denominator before you can get anywhere with adding or subtracting.

Q7 Add the following, simplifying your answers:

a) $\dfrac{3}{2x} + \dfrac{y}{2x}$

e) $\dfrac{3x+2}{x} + \dfrac{2x+4}{x}$

i) $\dfrac{2x}{3} + \dfrac{2x}{4}$

b) $\dfrac{1}{x} + \dfrac{y}{x}$

f) $\dfrac{6x}{3} + \dfrac{2x+y}{6}$

j) $\dfrac{x}{6} + \dfrac{5x}{7}$

c) $\dfrac{4xy}{3z} + \dfrac{2xy}{3z}$

g) $\dfrac{x}{8} + \dfrac{2+y}{24}$

k) $\dfrac{x}{3} + \dfrac{x}{y}$

d) $\dfrac{(4x+2)}{3} + \dfrac{(2x-1)}{3}$

h) $\dfrac{x}{10} + \dfrac{y-1}{5}$

l) $\dfrac{zx}{4} + \dfrac{x+z}{y}$

Q8 Subtract the following, leaving your answers as simplified as possible:

a) $\dfrac{4x}{3} - \dfrac{5y}{3}$

e) $\dfrac{10+x^2}{4x} - \dfrac{x^2+11}{4x}$

i) $\dfrac{2b}{a} - \dfrac{b}{7}$

b) $\dfrac{4x+3}{y} - \dfrac{4}{y}$

f) $\dfrac{2x}{3} - \dfrac{y}{6}$

j) $\dfrac{(p+q)}{2} - \dfrac{3p}{5}$

c) $\dfrac{(8x+3y)}{2x} - \dfrac{(4x+2)}{2x}$

g) $\dfrac{z}{5} - \dfrac{2z}{15}$

k) $\dfrac{p-2q}{4} - \dfrac{2p+q}{2}$

d) $\dfrac{(9-5x)}{3x} - \dfrac{(3+x)}{3x}$

h) $\dfrac{4m}{n} - \dfrac{m}{3}$

l) $\dfrac{3x}{y} - \dfrac{4-x}{3}$

Q9 Simplify the following:

a) $\left(\dfrac{a}{b} \div \dfrac{c}{d}\right) \times \dfrac{ac}{bd}$

d) $\dfrac{m^2n}{p} + \dfrac{mn}{p^2}$

g) $\dfrac{a+b}{a-b} + \dfrac{a-b}{a+b}$

b) $\dfrac{x^2+xy}{x} \times \dfrac{z}{xz+yz}$

e) $\dfrac{1}{x+y} + \dfrac{1}{x-y}$

h) $\dfrac{1}{4pq} \div \dfrac{1}{3pq}$

c) $\dfrac{(p+q)}{r} \times \dfrac{3}{2(p+q)}$

f) $\dfrac{2}{x} - \dfrac{3}{2x} + \dfrac{4}{3x}$

i) $\dfrac{x}{8} - \dfrac{x+y}{4} + \dfrac{x-y}{2}$

Solving Equations

Q1 When 1 is added to a number and the answer then trebled, it gives the same result as doubling the number and then adding 4. Find the number.

Q2 Solve the following:
  a) $2x^2 = 18$ **b)** $2x^2 = 72$ **c)** $3x^2 = 27$ **d)** $4x^2 = 36$ **e)** $5x^2 = 5$

Q3 Solve the following:
  a) $3x + 1 = 2x + 6$ **c)** $5x - 1 = 3x + 19$ **e)** $x + 15 = 4x$
  b) $4x + 3 = 3x + 7$ **d)** $x + 2 = \frac{1}{2}x - 1$ **f)** $3x + 3 = 2x + 12$

Q4 Solve the following:
  a) $3x - 8 = 7$ **d)** $2x - 9 = 25$ **f)** $5x - 2 = 6x - 7$
  b) $2(x - 3) = -2$ **g)** $30 - \frac{x^2}{2} = 28$
  c) $4(2x - 1) = 60$ **e)** $\frac{24}{x} + 2 = 6$

Q5 (x+1) cm A square has sides of length $(x + 1)$ cm. Find the value of x if:

  a) the perimeter of the square is 66 cm
  b) the perimeter of the square is 152.8 cm.

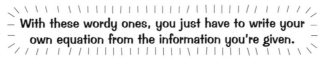

With these wordy ones, you just have to write your own equation from the information you're given.

Q6 Mr Smith sent his car to the local garage. He spent £x on new parts, four times this amount on labour and finally £29 for a safety test. If the total bill was for £106.50, find the value of x.

Q7 Solve:
  a) $2(x - 3) - (x - 2) = 5$ **g)** $\frac{x}{3} + 7 = 12$ **j)** $41 - \frac{x}{11} = 35$
  b) $5(x + 2) - 3(x - 5) = 29$
  c) $2(x + 2) + 3(x + 4) = 31$ **h)** $\frac{x}{10} + 18 = 29$ **k)** $\frac{x}{100} - 3 = 4$
  d) $10(x + 3) - 4(x - 2) = 7(x + 5)$
  e) $5(4x + 3) = 4(7x - 5) + 3(9 - 2x)$ **i)** $17 - \frac{x^2}{3} = 5$ **l)** $\frac{120}{x} = 16$
  f) $3(7 + 2x) + 2(1 - x) = 19$

Q8 Joan, Kate and Linda win £2400 on the lottery between them. Joan gets a share of £x, whilst Kate gets twice as much as Joan. Linda's share is £232 less than Joan's amount.
  a) Write down an expression for the amounts Joan, Kate and Linda win.
  b) Write down an equation in terms of x, and solve it.
  c) Write down the amounts Kate and Linda receive.

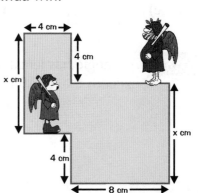

Q9 All the angles in the diagram are right angles.
  a) Write down an expression for the perimeter of the shape.
  b) Write down an expression for the area of the shape.
  c) For what value of x will the perimeter and area be numerically equal?

Solving Equations

Q10 Solve the following:

  a) $5(x - 1) + 3(x - 4) = -11$

  b) $3(x + 2) + 2(x - 4) = x - 3(x + 3)$

  c) $\dfrac{3x}{2} + 3 = x$

  d) $3(4x + 2) = 2(2x - 1)$

  e) $\dfrac{5x + 7}{9} = 3$

  f) $\dfrac{2x + 7}{11} = 3$

Q11 Two men are decorating a room. One has painted 20 m² and the other only 6 m². They continue painting and manage to paint another x m² each. If the first man has painted exactly three times the area painted by the second man, find the value of x.

Q12 Carol's father was 24 years old when Carol was born. Now he is four times as old as Carol. How old is Carol?

Q13 Mr Jones is 4 years older than his wife and 31 years older than his son. Their ages add up to 82 years. If Mr Jones is x years old, find the value of x and find the ages of his wife and son.

Q14 Solve the following:

  a) $\dfrac{y}{2} + 2 = 13$

  b) $\dfrac{3x}{4} - 2 = 4$

  c) $\dfrac{2z}{5} - 3 = -5$

  d) $\dfrac{1}{5}(x - 4) = 3$

  e) $\dfrac{2}{3}(x + 1) = 16$

  f) $\dfrac{3}{5}(4x - 3) = 15$

  g) $\dfrac{1}{4}x + \dfrac{1}{8}x = 1$

  h) $\dfrac{2}{3}x + \dfrac{4}{9}x = 20$

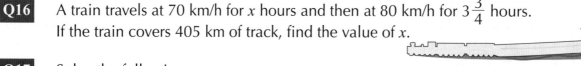

It's easy — you just put the 2 bits together and there's your equation. Then all you've got to do is solve it...

Q15 For what value of x is the expression $14 - \dfrac{x}{2}$ equal to the value $\dfrac{3x - 4}{2}$?

Q16 A train travels at 70 km/h for x hours and then at 80 km/h for $3\dfrac{3}{4}$ hours. If the train covers 405 km of track, find the value of x.

Q17 Solve the following:

Remember to do the same to the top and the bottom.

  a) $\dfrac{8}{x^2} = \dfrac{32}{36}$

  b) $\dfrac{12}{5x^2} = \dfrac{3}{20}$

  c) $\dfrac{14}{3x^2} = \dfrac{2}{21}$

  d) $\dfrac{4x + 3}{2} + x = \dfrac{5x + 41}{4}$

  e) $\dfrac{5}{7}(x - 2) - \dfrac{3}{4}(x + 3) = -4$

  f) $\dfrac{2x + 3}{2} - \dfrac{x - 2}{4} = \dfrac{4}{3}$

  g) $\dfrac{3x + 2}{5} + \dfrac{2(x - 3)}{10} = \dfrac{3}{2}$

  h) $\dfrac{x + 2}{6} - \dfrac{4 + 3x}{3} = \dfrac{7}{2}$

Q18 A triangle has lengths as shown below. Find the length of each side, if the length of AC exceeds that of AB by ½ cm.

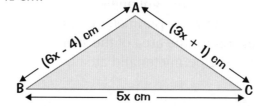

Rearranging Formulas

Rearranging is getting the letter you want out of the formula and making it the subject. And it's exactly the same method as for solving equations, which can't be bad.

Q1 Rearrange the following formulas to make the letter in brackets the new subject.

a) $g = 10 - 4h$ (h)

b) $d = \frac{1}{2}(c + 4)$ (c)

c) $j = -2(3 - k)$ (k)

d) $a = \frac{2b}{3}$ (b)

e) $f = \frac{3g}{8}$ (g)

f) $y = \frac{x}{2} - 3$ (x)

g) $s = \frac{t^3}{6} + 10$ (t)

h) $p = 4q^3$ (q)

Q2 Jason is saving up to go travelling next year and has got a temporary job selling cars. He is paid a basic wage of £500 a month, plus a bonus of £50 for each car he sells. He has a spreadsheet to keep track of his money, which calculates his wages (£w) after working for m months and selling c cars, using the following formula:
$$w = 500m + 50c$$
a) Rearrange the formula to make c the subject.
b) Find the number of cars Jason needs to sell in 11 months to earn £12 100.

Q3 The cost of hiring a car is £28 per day plus 25p per mile.
a) Find the cost of hiring the car for a day and travelling:

   i) 40 miles
   ii) 80 miles
b) Write down a formula to give the cost of hiring a car (£c) for one day, and travelling n miles.
c) Rearrange the formula to make n the subject.
d) How many miles can you travel, during one day, if you have a budget of:
   i) £34,   **ii)** £50,   **iii)** £56.50.

Q4 Rearrange the following formulas to make the letter in brackets the new subject.

a) $y = x^2 - 2$ (x)

b) $y = \sqrt{(x + 3)}$ (x)

c) $r = \left(\frac{s}{2}\right)^2$ (s)

d) $f = \frac{10 + g}{3}$ (g)

e) $w = \frac{5 - z}{2}$ (z)

f) $v = \frac{1}{3}x^2h$ (x)

g) $v^2 = u^2 + 2as$ (a)

h) $v^2 = u^2 + 2as$ (u)

i) $t = 2\pi\sqrt{\frac{l}{g}}$ (g)

Q5 Mrs Smith buys x jumpers for £J each and sells them in her shop for a total price of £T.
a) Write down an expression for the amount of money she paid for all the jumpers.
b) Using your answer to **a)**, write down a formula for the profit £P Mrs Smith makes selling all the jumpers.
c) Rearrange the formula to make J the subject.
d) Given that Mrs Smith makes a profit of £156 by selling 13 jumpers for a total of £364, find the price she paid for each jumper originally.

Rearranging Formulas

Q6 A website offering digital photo printing charges 12p per print plus 60p postage.
a) Find the cost of ordering:
   i) 12 prints.
   ii) 24 prints.
b) Write down a formula for the cost C, in pence, of ordering x prints.
c) Rearrange the formula to make x the subject.
d) A regular customer is looking through old receipts to check she has
   been charged the right amount. How many prints should she have
   received in each of her last three transactions if she was charged:
   i) £4.92
   ii) £6.36
   iii) £12.12.

Q7 Rearrange the following formulas, by collecting terms in x and looking for common
factors, to make x the new subject.
a) $xy = z - 2x$
b) $ax = 3x + b$
c) $4x - y = xz$
d) $xy = 3z - 5x + y$
e) $xy = xz - 2$
f) $2(x - y) = z(x + 3)$
g) $xyz = x - y - wz$
h) $3y(x + z) = y(2z - x)$

Q8 Rearrange the following to make the letter in brackets the new subject.

a) $pq = 3p + 4r - 2q$ (p)

b) $fg + 2e = 5 - 2g$ (g)

c) $a(b - 2) = c(b + 3)$ (b)

d) $pq^2 = rq^2 + 4$ (q)

e) $4(a - b) + c(a - 2) = ad$ (a)

f) $\dfrac{x^2}{3} - y = x^2$ (x)

g) $\sqrt{hk^2 - 14} = k$ (k)

h) $2\sqrt{x} + y = z\sqrt{x} + 4$ (x)

i) $\dfrac{a}{b} = \dfrac{1}{3}(b - a)$ (a)

j) $\dfrac{m + n}{m - n} = \dfrac{3}{4}$ (m)

k) $\sqrt{\dfrac{(d - e)}{e}} = 7$ (e)

l) $\dfrac{x - 2y}{xy} = 3$ (y)

These are getting quite tricky — you've got to **collect like terms**, before you can make anything else the subject.

Q9 Rearrange the following formulas to make y the new subject.

a) $x(y - 1) = y$

b) $x(y + 2) = y - 3$

c) $x = \dfrac{y^2 + 1}{2y^2 - 1}$

d) $x = \dfrac{2y^2 + 1}{3y^2 - 2}$

Inequalities

Yet another one of those bits of Maths that looks worse than it is —
these are just like equations, really, except for the symbols.

Q1 Write down the inequality represented by each diagram below.

a)
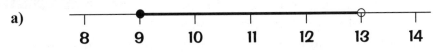

b)
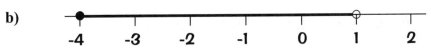

c)
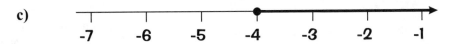

d)
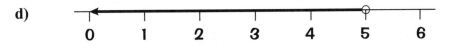

e)
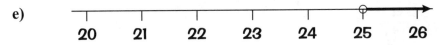

f)
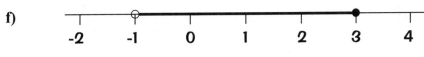

g)
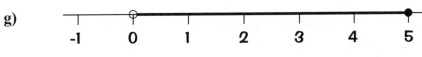

h)
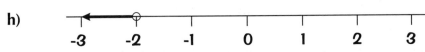

Q2 By drawing an appropriate part of the number line for each question, represent each of the following inequalities.

a) $x > 5$
b) $x \le 2$

c) $2 > x > -5$
d) $3 > x \ge -2$

e) $3 \ge x > -2$
f) $7 \ge x > 6$

g) $-3 \le x \le -2$
h) $0 \ge x > -3$

Q3 Solve the following:

a) $3x + 2 > 11$
b) $5x + 4 < 24$
c) $5x + 7 \le 32$
d) $3x + 12 \le 30$

e) $2x - 7 \ge 8$
f) $17 + 4x < 33$
g) $2(x + 3) < 20$
h) $2(5x - 4) < 32$

i) $5(x + 2) \ge 25$
j) $4(x - 1) > 40$
k) $10 - 2x > 4x - 8$
l) $7 - 2x \le 4x + 10$

m) $8 - 3x \ge 14$
n) $16 - x < 11$
o) $16 - x > 1$
p) $12 - 3x \le 18$

Q4 Find the largest integer x, such that $2x + 5 \ge 5x - 2$.

Q5 When a number is subtracted from 11, and this new number is then divided by two, the result is always less than five. Write this information as an inequality and solve it to show the possible values of the number.

Inequalities

Q6 Two schools are merging and a new school is being built to accommodate all the pupils. There will be 1130 pupils in total in the new school. No class must have more than 32 pupils. Show this information as an inequality. How many classrooms are needed?

> Call the number of classrooms x.

Q7 A couple are planning their wedding. For the reception in a local hotel, they have a budget of £900. If the hotel charges £18 per head, how many guests could be invited? Show this information as an inequality.

Q8 The shaded region satisfies three inequalities. Write down these inequalities.

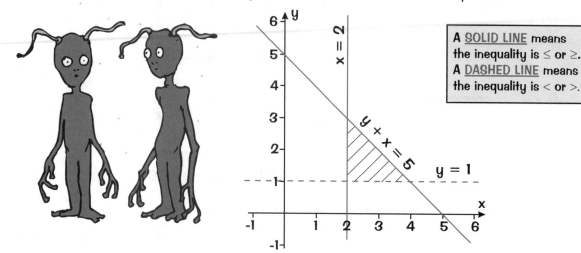

> A SOLID LINE means the inequality is $\leq$ or $\geq$.
> A DASHED LINE means the inequality is $<$ or $>$.

Q9 Draw a set of axes with the x-axis from –2 to 6 and the y-axis from –1 to 7. Show on a graph the region enclosed by the following three inequalities.

$$y < 6, \qquad x + y \geq 5 \qquad \text{and} \qquad x \leq 5$$

Q10 Draw and label a number line from –5 to 5 for each of the following inequalities. Represent the inequalities on your number lines.

a) $x^2 \leq 4$ **c)** $x^2 \leq 9$ **e)** $16 \geq x^2$ **g)** $9 > x^2$
b) $x^2 < 1$ **d)** $25 \geq x^2$ **f)** $x^2 \leq 1$ **h)** $x^2 \leq 0$

Q11 Draw a set of axes with the x-axis from –4 to 5 and the y-axis from –3 to 6. Show on a graph the region enclosed by the following.

$$y \leq 2x + 4, \qquad y < 5 - x \qquad \text{and} \qquad y \geq \frac{x}{3} - 1$$

Q12 A company are recruiting new members of staff. All applicants must take two online tests. To get an interview, applicants must score higher than 5 on the first test, at least 7 on the second, and have a total combined score of at least 14.

a) Write out three inequalities to represent the three criteria for getting an interview. Use x for the score on the first test and y for the score on the second test.

b) The company want to analyse the quality of applicants by plotting their test scores on a graph, and picking out the ones who satisfy the criteria. Using suitable axes, show on a graph the region enclosed by the three inequalities where suitable candidates would be placed.

Factorising Quadratics

Q1 Factorise the quadratics first, and then solve the equations:

a) $x^2 + 3x - 10 = 0$

b) $x^2 - 5x + 6 = 0$

c) $x^2 - 2x + 1 = 0$

d) $x^2 - 4x + 3 = 0$

e) $x^2 - x - 20 = 0$

f) $x^2 - 4x - 5 = 0$

g) $x^2 + 6x - 7 = 0$

h) $x^2 + 14x + 49 = 0$

i) $x^2 - 2x - 15 = 0$.

Q2 Rearrange into the form "$x^2 + bx + c = 0$", then solve by factorising:

a) $x^2 + 6x = 16$

b) $x^2 + 5x = 36$

c) $x^2 + 4x = 45$

d) $x^2 = 5x$

e) $x^2 = 11x$

f) $x^2 - 21 = 4x$

g) $x^2 - 300 = 20x$

h) $x^2 + 48 = 26x$

i) $x^2 + 36 = 13x$

j) $x + 5 - \dfrac{14}{x} = 0$

k) $x + 4 - \dfrac{21}{x} = 0$

l) $x(x - 3) = 10$

m) $x^2 - 3(x + 6) = 0$

n) $x - \dfrac{63}{x} = 2$

o) $x + 1 = \dfrac{12}{x}$

Q3 Solve $x^2 - \dfrac{1}{4} = 0$.

Q4 The area of a rectangular swimming pool is 28 m². The width is x m. The difference between the length and width is 3 m. Find the value of x.

x m

Q5 A rug has length x m. The width is exactly 1 m less than the length.

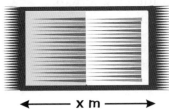

x m

a) Write down an expression for the area of the rug.

b) If the area of the rug is 6 m², find the value of x.

Q6 A triangle has height $(x + 1)$ cm and a base of $2x$ cm.

a) Write an expression for the area of the triangle and simplify it.

b) If the area of the triangle is 12 cm², find the value of x.

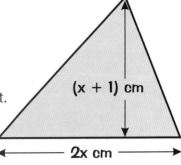

(x + 1) cm

2x cm

Q7 A square room has a floor of sides x metres.
The height of the walls is 3 m. Write down an expression for:

a) the floor area

b) the area of all four walls.

c) If the total area of the floor and the four walls is 64 m², form a quadratic equation and solve it to find x.

Factorising Quadratics

Q8   Factorise the quadratics first, and then solve the equations:

a) $2x^2 - 5x - 12 = 0$

b) $12x^2 - 17x - 5 = 0$

c) $2x^2 - x - 36 = 0$

d) $24x^2 - 34x + 12 = 0$

e) $6x^2 - 2x - 4 = 0$

f) $4x^2 + 3x - 10 = 0$

g) $10x^2 - 17x + 3 = 0$

h) $9x^2 - 3x - 6 = 0$

i) $5x^2 + 4x - 12 = 0.$

Q9   Rearrange into the form "$x^2 + bx + c = 0$", then solve by factorising:

a) $3x^2 = 2 + x$

b) $4x(x - 2) = -3$

c) $2x(10x + 9) + 4 = 0$

d) $6x^2 = 18x$

e) $3(2x^2 + 3x - 5) = 0$

f) $7x + 5 = \dfrac{2}{x}$

g) $15x = 22 - \dfrac{8}{x}$

h) $5x + 16 + \dfrac{3}{x} = 0$

i) $6x^2 = 8(x + 1)$

Q10   These two shapes have equal areas. Find the value of x.

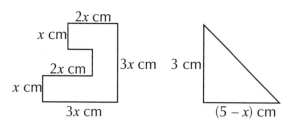

Q11   A photo has a length of l cm. Its width is $\frac{3}{4}$ cm shorter than the length.

a) Write down an expression for the area of the photo.

b) The photo is enlarged using a scale factor of 4.

   i)   Write an expression for the area of the enlarged photo.

   ii)   The area of the enlarged photo is 340 cm².
     Work out the value of l.

Q12   Simplify the following fractions by factorising first.

a) $\dfrac{4x + 12}{x^2 + 8x + 15}$

b) $\dfrac{x^2 + 2x}{x^2 - x - 6}$

c) $\dfrac{2x^2 - 12x}{x^2 - 3x - 18}$

d) $\dfrac{x^2 - 3x + 2}{xy - 2y}$

e) $\dfrac{(x + 2)^2}{x^2 - x - 6}$

f) $\dfrac{2x^2 + 7x + 3}{2x^2 - x - 1}$

g) $\dfrac{6x^2 + x - 1}{3x^2 + 5x - 2}$

h) $\dfrac{2x^2 + x - 3}{2x^2 + 9(x + 1)}$

i) $\dfrac{6(x^2 - 2) + x}{9(x^2 - x) - 4}$

The Quadratic Formula

Q1 Find the two values, to 2 d.p., given by each of the following expressions:

a) $\dfrac{2 \pm \sqrt{3}}{2}$

b) $\dfrac{4 \pm \sqrt{10}}{3}$

c) $\dfrac{-2 \pm \sqrt{27}}{2}$

d) $\dfrac{-3 \pm \sqrt{42}}{3}$

e) $\dfrac{-10 \pm \sqrt{160}}{5}$

f) $\dfrac{-27 \pm \sqrt{10}}{2}$

g) $\dfrac{-8 \pm \sqrt{9.5}}{2.4}$

h) $\dfrac{10 \pm \sqrt{88.4}}{23.2}$

Q2 The following quadratics can be solved by factorisation, but practise using the formula to solve them.

a) $x^2 + 8x + 12 = 0$
b) $6x^2 - x - 2 = 0$
c) $x^2 - x - 6 = 0$
d) $x^2 - 3x + 2 = 0$
e) $4x^2 - 15x + 9 = 0$
f) $x^2 - 3x = 0$
g) $36x^2 - 48x + 16 = 0$
h) $3x^2 + 8x = 0$
i) $2x^2 - 7x - 4 = 0$

j) $x^2 + x - 20 = 0$
k) $4x^2 + 8x - 12 = 0$
l) $3x^2 - 11x - 20 = 0$
m) $x + 3 = 2x^2$
n) $5 - 3x - 2x^2 = 0$
o) $1 - 5x + 6x^2 = 0$
p) $3(x^2 + 2x) = 9$
q) $x^2 + 4(x - 3) = 0$
r) $x^2 = 2(4 - x)$

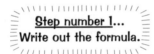

Step number 1...
Write out the formula.

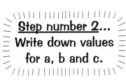

Step number 2...
Write down values
for a, b and c.

Step number 3... sub a, b and c into the formula. Make sure
you divide the **whole** of the top line by **2a** — not just ½ of it.

Q3 Solve the following quadratics using the formula. Give your answers to no more than two decimal places.

a) $x^2 + 3x - 1 = 0$
b) $x^2 - 2x - 6 = 0$
c) $x^2 + x - 1 = 0$
d) $x^2 + 6x + 3 = 0$
e) $x^2 + 5x + 2 = 0$
f) $x^2 - x - 1 = 0$
g) $3x^2 + 10x - 8 = 0$

h) $x^2 + 4x + 2 = 0$
i) $x^2 - 6x - 8 = 0$
j) $x^2 - 14x + 11 = 0$
k) $x^2 + 3x - 5 = 0$
l) $7x^2 - 15x + 6 = 0$
m) $2x^2 + 6x - 3 = 0$
n) $2x^2 - 7x + 4 = 0$

Oops, forgot to mention step number 4...
check your answers by putting them 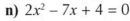 back in the equation.

The Quadratic Formula

Q4 Rearrange the following in the form "$ax^2 + bx + c = 0$" and then solve by the quadratic formula. Give your answers to two decimal places.

a) $x^2 = 8 - 3x$

b) $(x + 2)^2 - 3 = 0$

c) $3x(x - 1) = 5$

d) $2x(x + 4) = 1$

e) $x^2 = 4(x + 1)$

f) $(2x - 1)^2 = 5$

g) $3x^2 + 2x = 6$

h) $(x + 2)(x + 3) = 5$

i) $(x - 2)(2x - 1) = 3$

j) $2x + \dfrac{4}{x} = 7$

k) $\left(x - \dfrac{1}{2}\right)^2 = \dfrac{1}{4}$

l) $4x(x - 2) = -3$

 Pythagoras... remember him — you know, that bloke who didn't like angles.

Q5 The sides of a right-angled triangle are as shown. Use Pythagoras' theorem to form a quadratic equation in x and then solve it to find x.

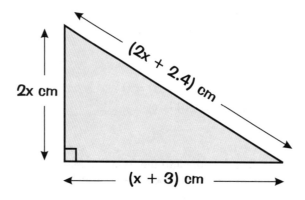

2x cm

(2x + 2.4) cm

(x + 3) cm

Q6 The area of a rectangle with length $(x + 4.6)$ cm and width $(x - 2.1)$ cm is 134.63 cm².

a) Form a quadratic equation and solve it to find x to two decimal places.

b) What is the rectangle's perimeter to one decimal place?

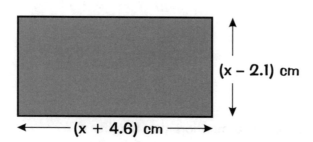

(x – 2.1) cm

(x + 4.6) cm

Simultaneous Equations and Graphs

Q1 Solve the following simultaneous equations by drawing graphs. Use values $0 \leqslant x \leqslant 6$.

a) $y = x$
$y = 9 - 2x$

b) $y = 2x + 1$
$2y = 8 + x$

c) $y = 4 - 2x$
$x + y = 3$

d) $y = 3 - x$
$3x + y = 5$

e) $2x + y = 6$
$y = 3x + 1$

f) $y = 2x$
$y = x + 1$

g) $x + y = 5$
$2x - 1 = y$

h) $2y = 3x$
$y = x + 1$

i) $y = x - 3$
$y + x = 7$

j) $y = x + 1$
$2x + y = 10$

Q2 The diagram shows the graphs:
$y = x^2 - x$
$y = x + 2$
$y = 8$
$y = -2x + 4$

Use the graphs to find the solutions (to 1 d.p.) to:

a) $x^2 - x = 0$

b) $x^2 - x = 8$

c) $x^2 - x - 8 = 0$

d) $x^2 - x = x + 2$

e) $x^2 - 2x - 2 = 0$

f) $x^2 - x = -2x + 4$

g) $x^2 + x - 4 = 0$

h) $-2x + 4 = x + 2$

i) $-3x + 2 = 0$

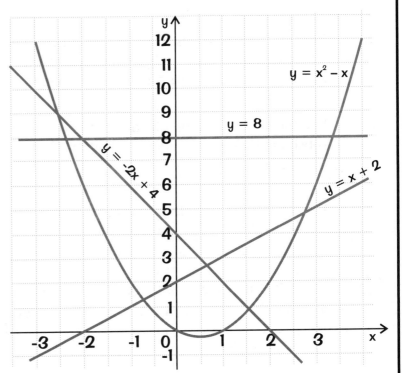

 These equations look a bit nasty, but they're just made up of the equations you've got graphs for. And you know how to do the rest of it, don't you...

Q3 Complete this table for $y = -\dfrac{1}{2}x^2 + 5$:

x	-4	-3	-2	-1	0	1	2	3	4
-½ x²									
y = -½ x²+5									

Draw the graph $y = -\dfrac{1}{2}x^2 + 5$.
Use your graph to solve the following equations (to 1 d.p.):

a) $-\dfrac{1}{2}x^2 + 5 = 0$

b) $-\dfrac{1}{2}x^2 + 8 = 0$

c) $-\dfrac{1}{2}x^2 - x + 5 = 0$

Simultaneous Equations

To solve simultaneous equations from scratch, you've got to get rid of
either x or y first — to leave you with an equation with just one unknown in it.

Q1 Solve the following simultaneous equations:

a) $3x = y$
$x - y = -4$

b) $2y = x$
$y + x = 24$

c) $y = 4x$
$x - y = 12$

Q2 Find the value of x and y for each of the following rectangles, by first
writing down a pair of simultaneous equations and then solving them.

a)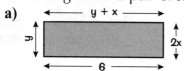

b)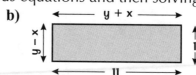

Q3 Isobel is buying sweets. She weighs out 20 jellies and 30 toffees, which come to 230 g.
She takes one of each off the scales before they get bagged up, and the weight drops to
221 g. How much does an individual toffee weigh?

Q4 Use the linear equation (the one with no x^2s in it) to find an expression for y. Then
substitute it into the quadratic equation (the one <u>with</u> x^2s in it), to solve these equations:

a) $y = x^2 + 2$
$y = x + 14$

b) $y = x^2 - 8$
$y = 3x + 10$

c) $y = 2x^2$
$y = x + 3$

d) $x + 5y = 30$
$x^2 + \frac{4}{5}x = y$

e) $y = 1 - 13x$
$y = 4x^2 + 4$

f) $y = 3(x^2 + 3)$
$14x + y = 1$

g) $y^2 + x^2 = 20$
$y = 3x + 2$

h) $y^2 + x^2 = 9$
$y + 2x = 3$

Q5 Solve the following simultaneous equations:

a) $4x + 6y = 16$
$x + 2y = 5$

b) $y = x^2 - 2$
$y = 3x + 8$

c) $\frac{x}{2} - 2y = 5$
$12y + x - 2 = 0$

d) $x + y = \frac{1}{2}(y - x)$
$x + y = 2$

Q6 Two farmers are buying livestock at a market. Farmer Ed buys 6 sheep and 5 pigs
for £430 and Farmer Jacob buys 4 sheep and 10 pigs for £500.

a) If sheep cost £x and pigs cost £y, write down the
two purchases as a pair of simultaneous equations.

b) Solve for x and y.

Q7 Two customers enter a shop to buy milk and cornflakes. Mrs Smith buys 5 pints of milk
and 2 boxes of cornflakes and spends £3.44. Mr Brown buys
4 pints of milk and 3 boxes of cornflakes and receives £6.03
change after paying with a £10 note. Write down a pair of
simultaneous equations and solve them to find the price in
pence of a pint of milk (m) and a box of cornflakes (c).

Q8 Solve $\dfrac{3(x - y)}{5} = x - 3y = x - 6$.

Direct and Inverse Proportion

Q1 y is directly proportional to x. If $y = 5$ when x is 25, find y when x is 100.

Q2 y is directly proportional to x. If y is 1.2 when x is 2.5, find the value of y when $x = 3.75$.

Q3   Complete the following tables of values where y is always directly proportional to x.

a)

X	2	4	6
y	5	10	

b)

X	3	6	9
y		9	

c)

X	27		
y	5	10	15

Q4   If $y = 3$ when $x = 8$ and y is inversely proportional to x, find the value of y when $x = 12$.

Q5   If y and x vary inversely, and $y = 12$ when $x = 3$ find:
a) the value of x when $y = 9$
b) the value of y when $x = 6$.

Q6   The length of a squid is proportional to the number of raccoons it has eaten.
A squid 890 cm long was found to have eaten 58 raccoons in its lifetime. Calculate:
a) the length of a squid that had eaten 29 raccoons
b) the number of raccoons a 614 cm long squid has eaten.

Q7   Some scientists are building a telescope to view a space dragon.
They know the length is proportional to the magnification and calculate that
a telescope 3 metres long will make the dragon appear 50 times larger.
a) How long would it need to be to make the dragon appear:
   i) 75 times larger?   **ii)** 220 times larger?
b) They find the space dragon looks too scary so close up.
How long does the telescope need to be to make the dragon appear 15 times larger?

Q8   If $y \propto x$ and $y = 132$ when $x = 10$, find the value of y when $x = 14$.

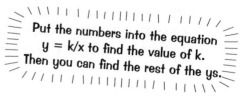

Q9   If $y \propto x$ and $y = 117$ when $x = 45$, find the value of x when $y = 195$.

Q10   If $y \propto \dfrac{1}{x}$ and $x = 4$ when $y = 5$, find the value of x when $y = 10$.

Q11   Given that $y \propto \dfrac{1}{x}$, complete this table of values.

x	1	2	3	4	5	6
y					9.6	

> Put the numbers into the equation $y = k/x$ to find the value of k. Then you can find the rest of the ys.

Make sure you know the 4 main details about Direct and Inverse Proportion:
1) what happens when one quantity increases,
2) the graph,
3) the table of values,
4) whether it's the ratio or the product that's the same for all values.

Direct and Inverse Proportion

Q12 If $y \propto x^2$ and $y = 4$ when $x = 4$, find the value of y when $x = 12$.

Q13 $y = kx^3$ and $y = 200$ when $x = 5$.
a) Find the value of k.
b) Find the value of y when $x = 8$.
c) Find the value of x when $y = 2433.4$.

Q14 Given that y varies inversely as the square of x, complete the following table of values, given that x is always positive.

X	1	2	5	
y			4	1

X	2			8
y	24	6	2⅔	

Q15 Two cylindrical containers are filled to the same depth, d cm, with water. The mass of the water in each container is proportional to the square of the radius of each container. The first container has a radius of 16 cm and the water has a mass of 16 kg. If the second container has a radius of 8 cm, find the mass of the water inside it.

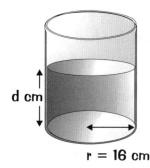

d cm

r = 16 cm

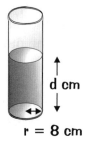

d cm

r = 8 cm

Q16 Given that r varies inversely as the square of s, and $r = 24$ when $s = 10$, find the values of:
a) r when $s = 5$
b) s when $r = 150$, given that s is positive
c) r when $s = 2$
d) s when $r = 37\frac{1}{2}$, given that s is negative

Don't forget about that little joker, the "inverse square" variation — they'll expect you to know that, too.

Q17 The gravitational pull of the Earth is inversely proportional to the square of the distance from the centre of the Earth. At the Earth's surface (approx. 6370 km from the centre) the gravitational pull is around 9.8 N kg⁻¹. When launching a satellite into space, the gravitational pull helps determine the orbit. What would be the gravitational pull on a satellite at a height of 100 km above the Earth's surface (to 1 d.p.)?

Q18 By considering the values in the table, decide whether $y \propto x$, $y \propto \frac{1}{x}$ or $y \propto \frac{1}{x^2}$.
a) Write down the equation which shows how y varies with x.
b) Find the value of y when $x = 6.4$.
c) Find the value of x when $y = 16$.

X	1.2	2.5	3.2	4.8
y	166⅔	80	62.5	41⅔

Sequences

Q1 For each of the sequences below, write down the next three numbers and the rule that you used.

a) 1, 3, 5, 7,...

b) 2, 4, 8, 16,...

c) 3, 30, 300, 3000,...

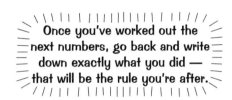

Once you've worked out the next numbers, go back and write down exactly what you did — that will be the rule you're after.

d) 3, 7, 11, 15,...

e) 19, 14, 9, 4, –1,...

Q2 For the following, use the rule given to generate the first 5 terms of the sequence.

a) $3n + 1$, when $n = 1, 2, 3, 4$ and 5.

b) $5n – 2$, when $n = 1, 2, 3, 4$ and 5.

c) n^2, when $n = 1, 2, 3, 4$ and 5.

d) $n^2 – 3$, when $n = 1, 2, 3, 4$ and 5.

Q3 10, 20, 15, 17½, 16¼...
a) Write down the next 4 terms.
b) Explain how you would work out the 10th term.

Q4 Write down an expression for the nth term of the following sequences:
a) 2, 4, 6, 8, …
b) 1, 3, 5, 7, …
c) 5, 10, 15, 20, …
d) 5, 8, 11, 14, …

Sequences

Q5   In the following sequences, write down the next 3 terms and the *n*th term:

a) 7, 10, 13, 16,...

c) 6, 16, 26, 36,...

b) 12, 17, 22, 27,...

d) 54, 61, 68, 75,...

Q6

The pattern above is based on individual triangles.
a) Write down the number of individual triangles in each group shown above.
b) Work out the number of individual triangles that would be in each of the next three groups.
c) Find a formula for the number of individual triangles in the *n*th term of the pattern.

> For the increasing/decreasing difference
> type questions, you've got to work out how
> much the difference changes each time.

Q7   Write down the next three terms and *n*th term of:

a) 5, 8, 12, 17,...

e) 729, 243, 81, 27,...

b) 6, 9, 14, 21,...

f) 31250, 6250, 1250, 250,...

c) 9, 12, 19, 30,...

g) 12288, 3072, 768, 192,...

d) 14, 19, 27, 38,...

h) 5103, 1701, 567, 189,...

Q8   Hannah is tiling her kitchen floor. She's making a square
pattern with grey and white tiles. In the centre there will
be a grey tile. The rest of the pattern will be made up of
alternating grey and white tiles, with the four corner tiles
of the square being grey.
Assume that *n* = 1 in the pattern shown opposite.

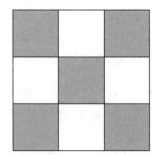

Work out, in terms of *n*, the formula for:
a) the number of grey tiles Hannah will need to buy
b) the number of white tiles she will need to buy
c) the total number of tiles needed.

Functions

Right, functions. Don't let appearances deceive you — treat them like the regular equations that you've seen loads of times before. Nothing to worry about here then.

Q1 Express the following equations using function notation:

a) $y = 3 + x$ b) $y = 790 - 41x$ c) $y = 3(9x^2 + 2)$

$f(x) = 3 + x$

Q2 For the following functions find x when $f(x) = 2$:

a) $f(x) = 2x - 7$ c) $f(x) = 5 - 4x \times 8x$ e) $f(x) = x^2 + 7x$
b) $f(x) = x^2 + 1$ d) $f(x) = 3x^2 - 10$ f) $f(x) = 252 - 2x^3$

Q3 For each of the following functions determine which values of x are excluded from the domain of f:

a) $f(x) = \sqrt{4 - x}$ c) $f(x) = (x - 1) \div x$ e) $f(x) = \dfrac{10}{4x + 3}$
b) $f(x) = x^{-\frac{1}{2}}$ d) $f(x) = \sqrt{2x + 7}$

Q4 If $f(x) = 4x + 12$ and $g(x) = 3 - x^2$ then find:

a) $f(8)$ c) $f(-4)$ e) $fg(x)$
b) $g(3)$ d) $gf(x)$ f) $gf(2)$

Q5 If $f(x) = \dfrac{11}{x + 1}$, $g(x) = \dfrac{3x}{4}$ and $h(x) = 6 + x$ then find:

a) $h^{-1}(x)$ c) $g^{-1}(h(x))$ e) $h^{-1}(f(5))$
b) $f^{-1}(x)$ d) $f^{-1}(g(x))$ f) $h^{-1}(g(-1))$

Q6 Evaluate the following:

a) $f(-1)$ where $f(x) = \dfrac{2 + 4x}{3}$ d) $n^{-1}(2)$ where $n(x) = 32 + 4(-x + 7)$

b) $g(9)$ where $g(x) = 7x^3 - 13$ e) $t: x \longrightarrow 21 - x^2$ where $x = 3$

c) $kj(-3)$ where $j(x) = \dfrac{6(x - 2)}{2}$ and $k(x) = -14x$ f) $v: x \longrightarrow -\dfrac{3x}{12}$ where $x = 3$

Q7 Find:

a) $hi(x)$, if $h(x) = \dfrac{11}{x^2} - 8$ and $i(x) = -x + \dfrac{x^2}{2}$

b) $m^{-1}(x)$, if $m(x) = \dfrac{18x - 12}{10} + 3$

c) $p^{-1}(q(x))$, if $p(x) = 8x + 5$ and $q(x) = \dfrac{13}{x - 2}$

D/T and S/T Graphs

You need to remember what the different bits of a travel graph mean — what it looks like when <u>stopped</u>, <u>changing speed</u> and <u>coming back</u> to the starting point.

Q1 Peter set out from A at 0900 to walk to B.
a) How far did he walk in the 1st hour?
b) He stopped twice; how long was each stop?
c) What was his speed after the second stop?

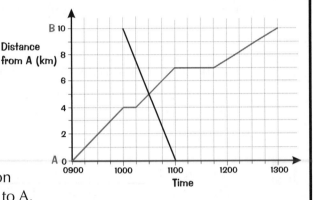

At 1000 Sarah set out on her bike to ride from B to A.
d) What time did she arrive at A?
e) What was her average speed?
f) At what time did Peter and Sarah pass each other?

Q2 Dave drives a bus from Kendal to Ingleton and back again. The bus company graphed the journey to help them organise their bus schedules.

a) How long did it take to get to Ingleton?
b) How much time was spent driving to and from Ingleton excluding stops?
c) What was the average speed for the journey from Kendal to Ingleton?
d) What was Dave's fastest speed?
e) The transport manager wants Dave to reduce the duration of the stops on the Kendal to Ingleton route so that he can make another journey from Kendal to Windermere starting at 1630. Would this be possible?

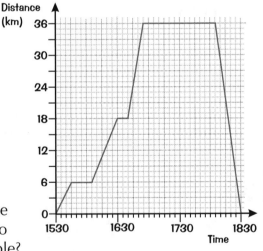

Q3 A train operator plans to purchase a new engine. They've graphed the journeys made by five engines over a 100 km stretch of track to help them decide which one is best.

a) Calculate the speed of each train and state which one was the fastest.
b) How could you tell by looking at the diagram which was the fastest and which was the slowest?

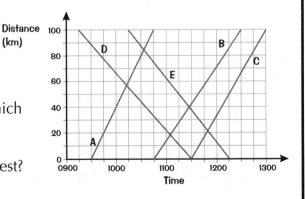

D/T and S/T Graphs

Q4   Mr Smith leaves home at 0730 to go to work. He walks at a steady 6 km/h for 2 km.
He catches the 0755 train, which takes 35 mins to travel 50 km. He then walks 3 km
to work and arrives at 0900.

Draw a graph to show this. How long did he wait at the station for the train?

Q5   This is a speed-time graph for part
of a cycle ride.

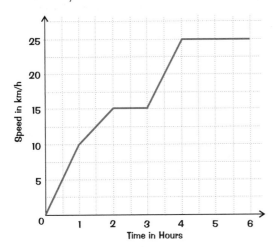

a) How long in total was the cyclist
accelerating for?
b) When was the cyclist travelling the fastest?
c) What does the graph show the cyclist was
doing in the third hour of the ride?

Q6   This is a speed-time graph of a
train journey.

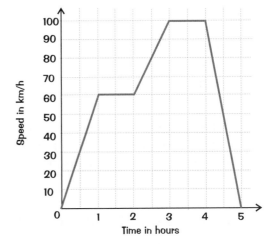

a) Calculate the acceleration of the
train in the third hour of the journey.
b) In which of the first four hours of the
journey was the train's acceleration
greatest?

Q7   Two cars start a journey at midday (1200) — one travels from town A to village B, and
the other from village B to town A. A and B are 80 km apart. The car from town A
travels at an average speed of 48 km/h and the other car, from village B, at 60 km/h.
a) Draw a graph to show these journeys.
b) At what time do the cars pass? (approx.)
c) Approximately how far from A are they when they pass?

> Use the speeds given to work
> out the time it takes for each
> car to travel the 80 km.

Q8   A girl set off on an all-day walk. She started at 0915 and walked at a steady speed for
9 km before stopping at 1100 for a 20 minute break. She then set off again at a steady
speed and walked 8 km, stopping at 1300 for 45 minutes. After lunch she walked at
3½ km/h for 2½ hours to her destination.
a) Draw a graph to show this walk.
b) How far did she walk altogether?
c) What was the average speed for the whole walk?
d) What was her fastest walking speed?

Conversion Graphs

Q1 This graph can be used to convert the distance (miles) travelled in a taxi to the fare payable (£).

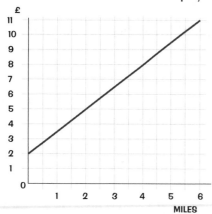

a) How much will the fare be if you travel:
  i) 2 miles?
  ii) 5 miles?
  iii) 10 miles?

b) Mike lives 4.5 miles away from his friend. Is £16 enough money for Mike to get a taxi to his friend's house and back?

Q2 The graph on the right can be used to give a rough conversion between US dollars ($) and British pounds (£). Use the graph to estimate:

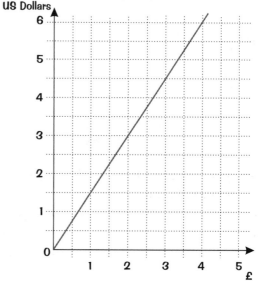

a) how many dollars you would get for £3

b) how many dollars you would get for £1.50

c) how many pounds you would get for $3

d) how many pounds you would get for $5.50.

Q3 80 km is roughly equal to 50 miles.
Use this information to draw a conversion graph on the grid.

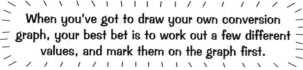

When you've got to draw your own conversion graph, your best bet is to work out a few different values, and mark them on the graph first.

a) Use the graph to estimate the number of miles equal to:
  i) 20 km
  ii) 70 km
  iii) 90 km

b) Use the graph to estimate how many km are equal to:
  i) 40 miles
  ii) 10 miles
  iii) 30 miles

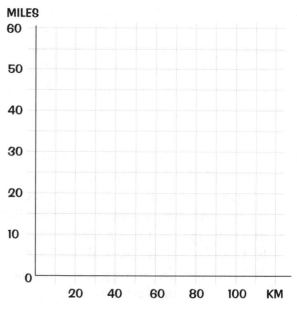

The Meaning of Area and Gradient

Q1 Describe the meaning of the gradient in each of the graphs below:

a)

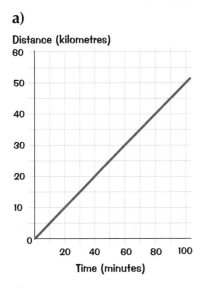

b)

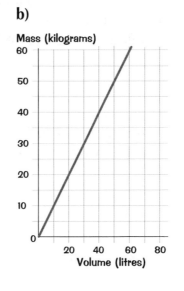

c)

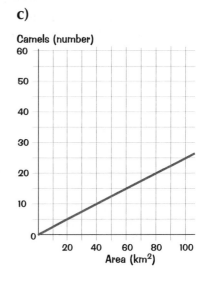

Add up all the little trapeziums to find the whole area — easy trapeasy...

Q2 This graph shows the volume of water in a swimming pool as it is filled.

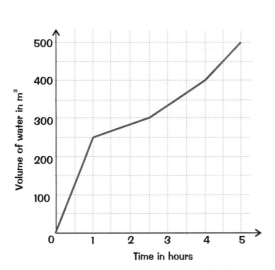

Calculate the flow rate of the water (in m³ per hour):

a) during the first hour

b) during the last hour.

Q3 This graph shows the speed of a train during a period of eight seconds.

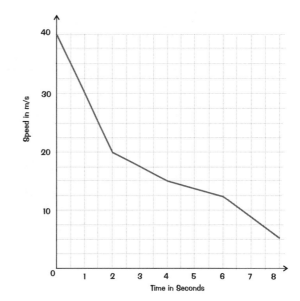

Estimate the total distance travelled in the period of eight seconds by dividing the area into four trapeziums of equal width.

Coordinates

Q1   ABCD is a <u>parallelogram</u>. A is (-1, 3), B is (-2, -1) and C is (4, -1).
Draw axes with x from -3 to 5 and y from -2 to 4.
Plot A, B and C then find the <u>missing coordinates</u> for D.

Q2   Draw axes with x from -9 to 9 and y from -12 to 12.
On the <u>same</u> set of axes draw the following shapes and find their
<u>missing pair of coordinates</u>.

a) ABCD is a <u>square</u>.
A is (1, 1)
B is ?
C is (-3, -3)
D is (-3, 1)

c) ABCD is a <u>rectangle</u>.
A is ?
B is (3, -8)
C is (3, -6)
D is (-5, -6)

e) ABCD is a <u>parallelogram</u>.
A is (-2, -10)
B is (4, -10)
C is (6, -12)
D is ?

b) ABCD is a <u>parallelogram</u>.
A is (2, 8)
B is (6, 8)
C is ?
D is (1, 5)

d) ABCD is a <u>kite</u>.
A is (-9, 3)
B is (-6, 8)
C is (-4, 8)
D is ?

f) ABCD is a <u>parallelogram</u>.
A is (-8, 10)
B is (-6, 10)
C is ?
D is (-5, 12)

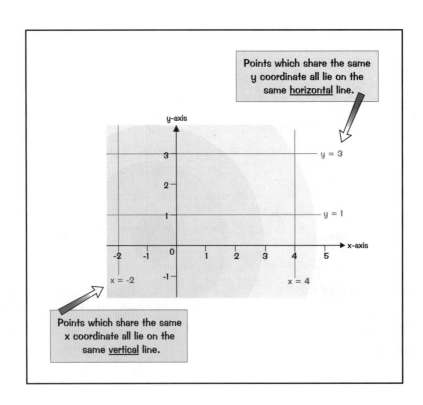

Points which share the same
y coordinate all lie on the
same <u>horizontal</u> line.

Points which share the same
x coordinate all lie on the
same <u>vertical</u> line.

Coordinates

Q3 ABCD is a <u>rectangle</u> with the line $x = 0$ as a <u>line of symmetry</u>.
Draw axes with x from -3 to 3 and y from -3 to 3.
If A = (-2, -2) and B is (-2, 1), find the <u>coordinates of C and D</u>.

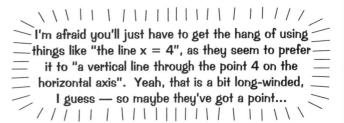
I'm afraid you'll just have to get the hang of using things like "the line x = 4", as they seem to prefer it to "a vertical line through the point 4 on the horizontal axis". Yeah, that is a bit long-winded, I guess — so maybe they've got a point...

Q4 Find the coordinates of the midpoint of the line segment AB.

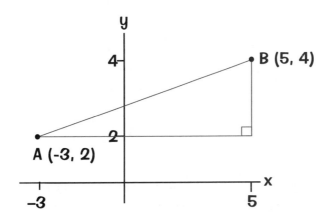

Q5 Find the midpoint of the line segment AB, where A and B have coordinates:

a) A(2, 3) B(4, 5)

b) A(1, 8) B(10, 2)

c) A(0, 11) B(11, 11)

d) A(3, 15) B(14, 3)

e) A(6, 7) B(0, 0)

f) A(16, 16) B(3, 3)

g) A(8, 33) B(32, 50)

h) A(17, 28) B(44, 13)

ahh... nice'n'easy...

Your answers should be coordinates too.

Q6 Anna is designing the plan of a kitchen using some computer-aided design software. The coordinates of the corners of the room on screen are (0, 10), (220, 10), (0, 260) and (220, 260). She needs to enter the coordinates of the ceiling light, which will be exactly in the centre of the room. What will the coordinates of the light be?

Straight Line Graphs

Q1 Which letters represent the following lines:

a) $x = y$
b) $x = 5$
c) $y = -x$
d) $x = 0$
e) $y = -7$
f) $x + y = 0$
g) $y = 5$
h) $x - y = 0$
i) $y = 0$
j) $x = -7$?

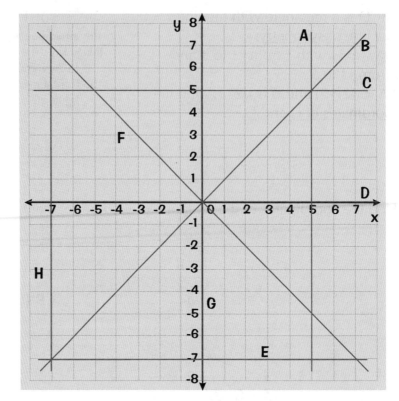

Don't get confused if you've got "x + y = ... " — just rearrange the equation to "y = -x + ..." and as if by magic, you've got a line you recognise.

Q2 Complete the following table for the line $y = 3x - 1$:

x	-4	-3	-2	-1	0	1	2	3	4
3x									
y = 3x – 1									

Plot these points on graph paper and hence draw the graph of $y = 3x - 1$.
Use a scale of 1 cm for 2 units on the *y*-axis and 2 cm for 1 unit on the *x*-axis.

Q3 Complete the following table for the line $y = \frac{1}{2}x - 3$:

x	-6	-4	-2	0	2	4	6
½x							
y = ½x – 3							

Plot these points on graph paper and hence draw the graph of $y = \frac{1}{2}x - 3$.

Straight Line Graphs

If you know it's a straight line, you only really need <u>two</u> points, but it's always a <u>good idea</u> to plot three — it's a bit of a safety net, really.

Q4 Complete this table of values for $y = 2x + 3$:

X	0	3	8
y			

Plot these points on graph paper and draw the graph of $y = 2x + 3$.
Use your graph to find:

a) The value of y when $x = 5$
b) The value of y when $x = 2$
c) The value of x when $y = 11$
d) The value of x when $y = 17$

Q5 Complete this table of values for $y = \frac{1}{4}x - 3$:

X	-8	-4	8
y			

Plot these points on graph paper and draw the graph of $y = \frac{1}{4}x - 3$.
Use your graph to find:

a) The value of y when $x = 2$
b) The value of y when $x = 0$
c) The value of x when $y = -2$
d) The value of x when $y = -1.5$

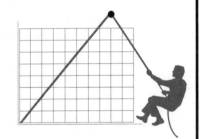

Q6 The cost of electricity is calculated using the formula:
Total cost = fixed charge + (cost per unit × number of units).
Customers can choose two different methods of payment:
Method A: fixed charge £10, cost per unit 25p
Method B: fixed charge £40, cost per unit 5p
Copy and complete this table:

Number of Units used	0	100	200	300
Cost using method A				
Cost using method B				

Plot these points on a graph (put the number of units on the horizontal axis, cost on the vertical axis):

a) Use your graph to find the total cost when 70 units are used for:
  i) Method A
  ii) Method B

b) Miss Wright used 75 units. Which method should she use to minimise her bill, Method A or Method B?

c) Use your graph to work out how many units Miss Wright would have to use for both methods to cost the same amount.

68

y = mx + c

 Writing the equation of a line in the form y = mx + c gives you a nifty way of finding the gradient and y-intercept. Remember that — it'll save you loads of time. Anything for an easy life...

Q1 What is the gradient of:
a) line segment A
b) line segment B
c) line segment C
d) line segment D
e) line segment E
f) line segment F
g) line segment G
h) line segment H
i) line segment I
j) line segment J
k) a line parallel to A
l) a line parallel to B
m) a line perpendicular to C?

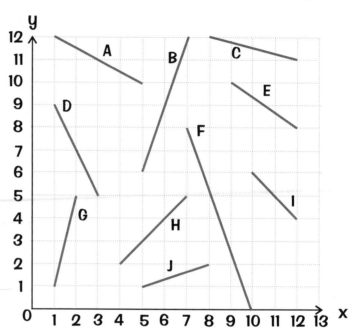

Uphill gradients are always positive, downhill always negative. Impressed? Hmmm... thought not. Can be a bit of an uphill battle, these.

Q2 What is the value of *x* or *y* if:
a) the point (*x*, 13) is on the line $y = 3x + 1$
b) the point (*x*, –2) is on the line $y = \frac{1}{2}x – 6$
c) the point (4, *y*) is on the line $y = 2x – 1$
d) the point (–3, *y*) is on the line $y = –3x$?

Q3 Which of the following points lie on the line $y = 3x – 1$?
(7, 20), (6, 15), (5, 14)

Q4 Lauren works in a ski resort grading ski runs. A blue run has a gradient less-steep than -0.2, a red run is steeper than a blue, but has a gradient shallower than -0.25. Anything steeper than a red run is a black run. A run is 1.75 km long and descends 400 metres. What colour should Lauren grade it?

Q5 For each of the following lines, give the gradient and the coordinates of the point where the line cuts the *y*-axis.
a) $y = 4x + 3$
b) $y = 3x – 2$
c) $y = 2x + 1$
d) $y = -3x + 3$
e) $y = 5x$
f) $y = -2x + 3$
g) $y = -6x – 4$
h) $y = x$
i) $y = -\frac{1}{2}x + 3$
j) $y = \frac{1}{4}x + 2$
k) $3y = 4x + 6$
l) $2y = -5x – 4$
m) $8y = 4x – 12$
n) $3y = 7x + 5$
o) $x + y = 0$
p) $x – y = 0$
q) $y – x = 3$
r) $x – 3 = y$
s) $y – 7 = 3x$
t) $y – 5x = 3$
u) $y + 2x + 3 = 0$
v) $y – 2x – 4 = 0$

 I know these are a bit algebra-ish, but don't worry, they won't bite.

SECTION FOUR — SEQUENCES, FUNCTIONS AND GRAPHS

y = mx + c

Q6 What is the gradient of the line joining the points:
a) (3, 5) and (5, 9)
b) (6, 3) and (10, 5)
c) (-6, 4) and (-3, 1)
d) (8, 2) and (4, 10)
e) (8, 5) and (6, 4)
f) (-3, -1) and (1, -4)?

Q7 Find the equations of the following lines:
a) A
b) B
c) C
d) D
e) E
f) F

Yeah, OK, this sounds a bit scary, but just work out the gradient (m) and look at the y-intercept (c) and pop them back into "y = mx + c"... easy lemons.

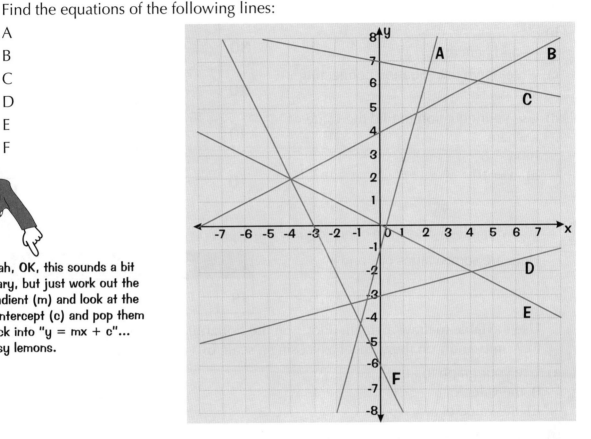

Q8 Find the equation of the straight line which passes through:
a) (3, 7) and has a gradient of 1
b) (2, 8) and has a gradient of 3
c) (–3, 3) and has a gradient of 2
d) (4, –4) and has a gradient of –1
e) (–1, 7) and has a gradient of –3
f) (4, –11) and has a gradient of –2.

Q9 Write down the equation of the straight line which passes through the points:
a) (2, 2) and (5, 5)
b) (1, 3) and (4, 12)
c) (–2, –3) and (5, 11)
d) (1, 0) and (5, –12)
e) (–5, 6) and (–1, –2)
f) (4, 23) and (–2, –7).

Here's a bit more practice with those gradients. Thought you'd like that.

SECTION FOUR — SEQUENCES, FUNCTIONS AND GRAPHS

Equations from Graphs

Q1 Two variables x and y are connected by the equation $y = mx + c$. Use the table to draw a graph with x on the horizontal axis and y on the vertical axis.

x	1	3	5	8
y	9	17	25	37

Use your graph to find the value of:

a) m

b) c
— and hence:

c) write down the equation connecting x and y.

d) Use your equation to find the value of y when:
  i) $x = 6$
  ii) $x = 10$

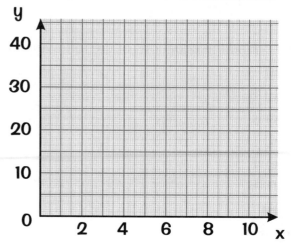

Q2 Two variables x and y are connected by the equation $y = ax + b$.

Here are some values of x and y.

x	4	9	16	25
y	5	7.5	11	15.5

Use the table to draw a graph. Plot x on the horizontal axis using a scale of 1 cm to 2 units and y on the vertical axis using a scale of 1 cm to 1 unit.

a) Use your graph to find:
  i) the value of a
  ii) the value of b.

b) Write down the equation connecting x and y.

Q3 CGPtronics semiconductor company plans to release a new microprocessor. It costs a certain amount to design, and a certain amount per unit to manufacture. The table below shows the total production cost for producing different numbers of microprocessors.

Units	10 000	30 000	50 000	70 000
Production cost	£23 000	£29 000	£35 000	£41 000

a) Plot the data from the table on a graph.

b) Use the graph to work out the cost of designing the microprocessor. Use this amount to work out the manufacturing cost per unit.

c) Write down an equation connecting the number of units made to the production cost.

d) CGPtronics want to sell the microprocessors for 80p each. On the same set of axes, plot a graph showing the revenue from selling different numbers of microprocessors.

revenue = value of sales

e) How many microprocessors will CGPtronics have to sell to break even?

Equations from Graphs

Q4 Dominic works in the finance office of a small company. He has been asked to review the company's energy costs, and is writing a report comparing two energy providers. The table below shows their prices, which vary with the amount of energy used.

Number of units used	100	200	300	500
Provider A price (£)	8	11	14	20
Provider B price (£)	5	10	15	25

Plot the points for both providers on the same graph with the number of units used on the horizontal axis and the price (£) on the vertical axis.

a) Find the formula connecting price (P) and number of units (N) used for each energy provider.

b) Use your formulas to calculate the price each energy provider would charge for:
   i) 400 units
   ii) 700 units.

c) Use the graph to determine the number of units the company would need to use for there to be no difference in price between the two providers.

Q5 The table shows the labour costs of having a television repaired. The cost consists of a fixed rate call-out charge plus a charge for each ten minutes.

Time (min)	10	20	30	40	50
Cost (£)	8	10		14	16

Plot the points on a graph with the time on the horizontal axis and the cost on the vertical axis.

a) Find a formula connecting the cost (C) in pounds and the time (M) in minutes.

b) What is the fixed rate call-out charge?

c) Use your graph to find the cost for 30 minutes.

d) Use your formula to find the cost for:
   i) 80 minutes
   ii) 100 minutes
   iii) 3 hours.

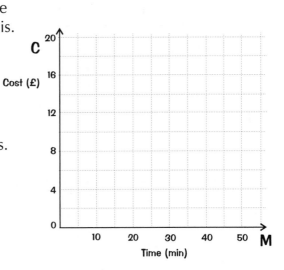

Graphs to Recognise

Q1 Identify the type of graph shown below.
Choose from straight line, quadratic, cubic and reciprocal:

a)
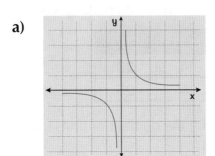

b)
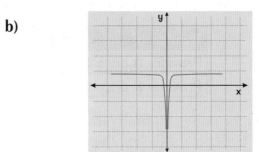

c)
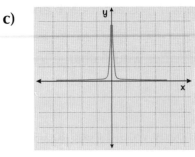

d)
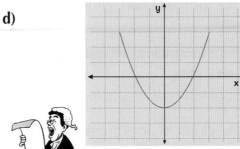

e)
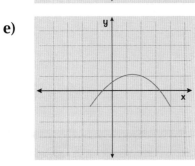

f)
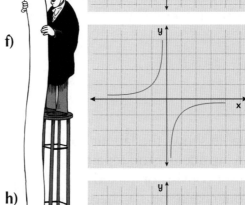

g)
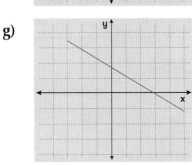

h)
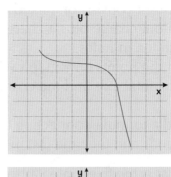

i)
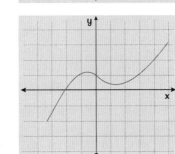

j)
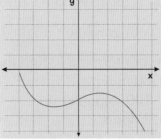

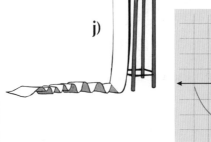

You'll need to be able to <u>sketch a graph</u> from <u>memory</u> — yeah, scary huh.
Don't worry — they only expect you to remember the <u>4 main ones</u> (phew) —
<u>straight line</u> (easy), <u>x²</u> (buckets), <u>x³</u> (wiggly) and <u>1/x</u> (2 bits and "x=0" missing).

Graphs to Recognise

Q2 Here are some equations, and there are some curves below. Match the equations to the curves.

a) $y = -2x - 1$

b) $y = 3x$

c) $y = x^2 + 2$

d) $y = -x^2 + 3$

e) $y = x^2$

f) $y = 2x^3 - 3$

g) $y = -\frac{1}{2}x^3 + 2$

h) $y = x^3$

i) $y = -\frac{3}{x}$

j) $y = \frac{2}{x}$

k) $y = \frac{1}{x^2}$

l) $y = -\frac{1}{x^2}$

i)

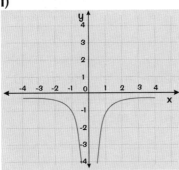

ii)
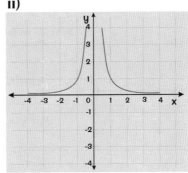

iii)
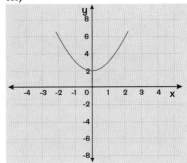

iv)
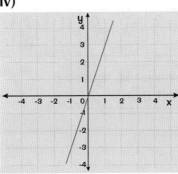

v)
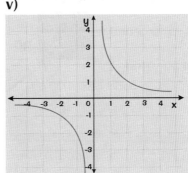

vi)
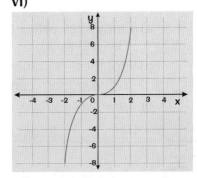

vii)
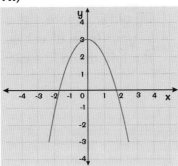

viii)
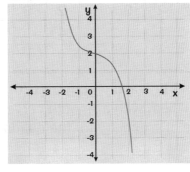

ix)
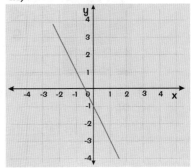

x)
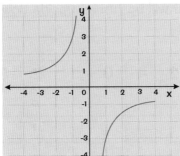

xi)
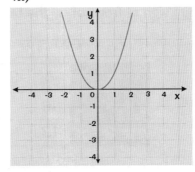

xii)
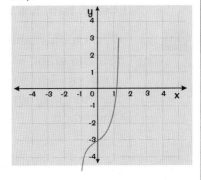

Quadratic Graphs

So, you can spot a quadratic graph at ten paces, but can you draw one...

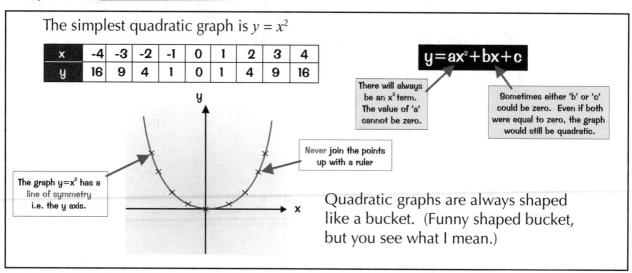

The simplest quadratic graph is $y = x^2$

x	-4	-3	-2	-1	0	1	2	3	4
y	16	9	4	1	0	1	4	9	16

$$y = ax^2 + bx + c$$

There will always be an x^2 term. The value of 'a' cannot be zero.

Sometimes either 'b' or 'c' could be zero. Even if both were equal to zero, the graph would still be quadratic.

Never join the points up with a ruler

The graph $y = x^2$ has a line of symmetry i.e. the y axis.

Quadratic graphs are always shaped like a bucket. (Funny shaped bucket, but you see what I mean.)

Q1 Complete this <u>table of values</u> for the quadratic graph $y = 2x^2$.

a) Draw axes with x from -5 to 5 and y from 0 to 32.

x	-4	-3	-2	-1	0	1	2	3	4
$y = 2x^2$	32	18					8		

Remember to square first then × 2

b) Plot these 9 points and join them with a <u>smooth curve</u>.

c) Label your graph.

Q2 Complete this table of values for the graph $y = x^2 + x$.

x	-4	-3	-2	-1	0	1	2	3	4
x^2	16	9					4		
$y = x^2 + x$	12					2			

By putting more steps in your table of values, the arithmetic is easier

a) Draw axes with x from -5 to 5 and y from 0 to 20.

b) Plot the points and join them with a smooth curve.

c) Draw and label the <u>line of symmetry</u> for the quadratic graph $y = x^2 + x$.

If the x^2 term has a <u>minus</u> sign in front of it, the bucket will be turned <u>upside down</u>.

Q3 a) Complete this table of values for the graph $y = 3 - x^2$.

b) Draw the graph $y = 3 - x^2$ for x from -4 to 4.

c) State the <u>maximum value</u> of the graph $y = 3 - x^2$.

x	-4	-3	-2	-1	0	1	2	3	4
$-x^2$	-16						-4		
$y = 3 - x^2$	-13						-1		

Cubic Graphs

You go about a cubic in the same way as you would a quadratic — but you should get a different shaped graph, of course. It's always a good idea to put <u>lots of steps</u> in the <u>table of values</u> — that way it's <u>easier to check</u> any points that look wrong.

Q1 Complete this table of values for $y = x^3$:

x	-3	-2	-1	0	1	2	3
y=x³							

Draw the graph of $y = x^3$.

Q2 Complete this table of values for $y = -x^3$:

x	-3	-2	-1	0	1	2	3
y=-x³							

Draw the graph of $y = -x^3$.

Q3 Complete this table of values for $y = x^3 + 4$:

x	-3	-2	-1	0	1	2	3
x³							
y=x³+4							

Draw the graph of $y = x^3 + 4$.

Remember — no rulers.

Q4 Complete this table of values for $y = -x^3 - 4$:

x	-3	-2	-1	0	1	2	3
-x³							
y=-x³-4							

Draw the graph of $y = -x^3 - 4$.

Q5 Look at your graphs for questions 1 and 3.
What has been done to graph 1 to change it into graph 3?
Without plotting a table of values draw the graph of $y = x^3 - 4$.

Q6 Look at your graphs for questions 2 and 4.
What has been done to graph 2 to change it into graph 4?
Without plotting a table of values draw the graph of $y = -x^3 + 4$.

Graphs of Other Equations

Here are some equations and shapes that are even more alien... Just go about doing them the same way as a cubic or quadratic and you'll be fine. Don't try to skip stages when you're working through it — **errors** will then become **much harder** to spot.

The two halves of a 1/x graph **never touch** and are **symmetrical** around y = x and y = -x.

Q1 Complete this <u>table of values</u> for the graph $y = 1/x$.

a) Draw axes with x from -4 to 4 and y from -1 to 1.

b) Plot these points and join them with a <u>smooth curve</u>.

c) Label your graph.

x	-4	-3	-2	-1	0	1	2	3	4
y=1/x		-0.33			n/a				0.25

The 0's just there to fool you — any equation with A/x in it never makes a graph that passes through x = 0.

A/x² graphs are similar to 1/x graphs but the two halves are **next to each other**.

Q2 Complete this table of values for the graph $y = 3/x^2$.

x	-4	-3	-2	-1	0	1	2	3	4
x²			0.25			1		0.11	
y=3/x²						3			

A is any number — positive or negative

a) Draw axes with x from -4 to 4 and y from 0 to 3.

b) Plot the points and join them with a smooth curve.

c) Draw and label the <u>line of symmetry</u> for the quadratic graph $y = 3/x^2$.

k^x graphs are always above the x-axis and pass through the point **(0, 1)**.

Q3 **a)** Complete this table of values for the graph $y = 2^x$.

b) Draw the graph $y = 2^x$ for x from -4 to 4.

c) Why do k^x graphs always pass through (0, 1)?

k is any positive number

x	-4	-3	-2	-1	0	1	2	3	4
y=2ˣ				0.5	1		4		

All these types of equations can be combined — see what shape of graph you get.

Q4 **a)** Complete this table of values for the graph $y = 3^x - 6/x$.

b) Draw the graph $y = 3^x - 6/x$ for x from -3 to 3.

x	-3	-2	-1	0	1	2	3
3ˣ			0.33		3		
6/x						3	
y=3ˣ – 6/x					-3		

Differentiation

Differentiation — not as nightmarish as it first looks.
It just takes a bit of practice and remembering that...

This bit just means 'the result of differentiating the thing in the brackets'.

$$\frac{d}{dx}(x^n) = nx^{n-1}$$

Q1 Find $\frac{dy}{dx}$ when:

a) $y = x^4$

b) $y = x^2$

c) $y = x^{13}$

d) $y = 2x^2$

e) $y = 5x^3$

f) $y = 7x^4$

g) $y = \frac{1}{2}x^4$

h) $y = 33x$

i) $y = x$

j) $y = 22$

k) $y = -3x^3$

l) $y = -\frac{1}{4}x^{16}$

Q2 Find:

a) $\frac{dy}{da}$ when $y = a^7$

b) $\frac{dy}{dt}$ when $y = 10t^5$

c) $\frac{dy}{ds}$ when $y = s$

d) $\frac{dy}{dw}$ when $y = -\frac{2}{3}w^6$

Q3 Find $\frac{dy}{dx}$ when:

a) $y = x^5 + 5$

b) $y = 2x^7 + 11$

c) $y = x + 2$

d) $y = 2x^2 + x$

e) $y = x^9 + 3x$

f) $y = 7x^3 + 6x^2$

g) $y = 4x^8 + x^2 + 3$

h) $y = 3x^5 + x^3 + x$

i) $y = \frac{1}{3}x^9 + x^5 + x^2 + 9$

Q4 Find $\frac{dy}{dx}$ when $y = 9x^4 + x^3 + 4x^2 + 6x + 22$

Q5 Find $\frac{dy}{dx}$ when $y = 3x^5 + 7x^4 + 8x^3 + 2x^2 + 10x + 13$

Q6 Find $\frac{dy}{dx}$ when $y = 5x^8 + 4x^6 + 12x^4 + 7x^2 + 8$

Q7 Find $\frac{dy}{dd}$ when $y = 11d^4 + 12d^3 + 9d^2 + 14d + 15$

Differentiation

Q8 Differentiate to get the gradient expression for the graphs of each of these equations.

a) $y = -4x^3 - x^2$

c) $y = -6x^3 - 2x^2 - 6$

e) $y = \dfrac{1}{x}$

b) $y = 5x^3 + 3x^2 + x$

d) $y = 2x^3 + x^2 - 8x + 3$

f) $y = \dfrac{1}{x^2}$

Q9 Find the gradient of each of these graphs at $x = 0.5$ by:

a) Drawing a tangent to the curve and finding its gradient.

b) Differentiation.

i)

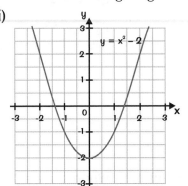

ii)

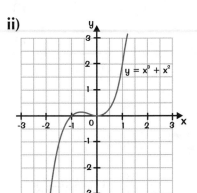

Q10 Find the gradient of the graph of each of the following equations at $x = -1$ and $x = 2$.

a) $y = -2x - 1$

d) $y = -x^2 + 3$

g) $y = -\dfrac{1}{2}x^3 + 2$

j) $y = \dfrac{2}{x}$

b) $y = 3x^3 + 2x^2$

e) $y = x^2$

h) $y = x^3$

k) $y = \dfrac{1}{x^2}$

c) $y = x^2 + 2$

f) $y = 2x^3 - 3$

i) $y = -\dfrac{3}{x}$

l) $y = -\dfrac{1}{x^2}$

Q11 Using differentiation to find gradients, decide which of the following is the graph of $y = x^3 + 3x^2 + x - 2$. Show your working.

A

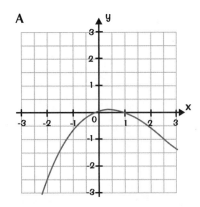

B

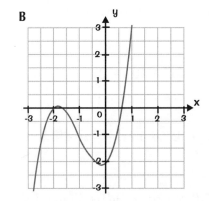

C

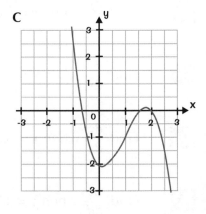

Differentiation

Q12 What are the coordinates of the point on the graph of
the equation $y = 2x^2 + 3x$ where the gradient is +11?

Q13 What are the coordinates of the point on the graph
of the equation $y = 4x^2 + 7$ where the gradient is +4?

Q14 The vertical distance, d, of a hot air balloon from the ground in km is given by the
formula $d = -t^2 + 3t$, where t is the time in hours and $0 \leq t \leq 3$.

a) For how long, to the nearest minute, is the hot air
balloon more than 1 km above the ground?

b) Find an expression for the vertical velocity of the balloon, v.

c) Find the vertical velocity of the balloon after 30 minutes and after 1 hour.

Q15 An object is fired from a space rocket. Its distance, d metres,
from a point O is given by the formula $d = 2t^2(t + 1)$, where t
is the number of seconds that have passed and $0 \leq t \leq 10$.

a) How far from point O is the object after 6 seconds?

b) Find the velocity of the object after 6 seconds.

c) Find the acceleration of the object after 6 seconds.

Q16 The velocity (in m/s) of a flying alien at time t seconds is given by the formula
$v = 4t^2 + 2t + 3$ (for $0 \leq t \leq 300$).

a) Find the velocity of the alien after 40 seconds.

b) Find the acceleration of the alien after 40 seconds.

Differentiation

Q17 Find the coordinates of the turning points of these graphs.
For each, say if the turning point is a maximum or minimum.

a) $y = 2x^2$

b) $y = 5x^2 + x$

c) $y = 3x^2 + 2x - 5$

d) $y = -x^2 + 4x - 8$

e) $y = (x + 4)(x - 8)$

Q18 Find $\dfrac{dy}{dx}$ for each of the following equations.

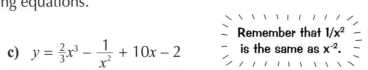

Remember that $1/x^2$ is the same as x^{-2}.

a) $y = x^4 - x^2 - 3x - 8$

b) $y = 4x^5 + 9x^4$

c) $y = \frac{2}{3}x^3 - \dfrac{1}{x^2} + 10x - 2$

d) $y = x^3 + 7.5x^2 + \dfrac{3}{x^4} + 1$

Q19 Find the coordinates of the turning points of the
graphs of each of the following equations.

a) $y = \frac{1}{3}x^3 - x^2 - 3x - 8$

b) $y = \frac{4}{3}x^3 - 16x^2 + 48x$

c) $y = \frac{2}{3}x^3 - 4.5x^2 - 5x - 2$

d) $y = x^3 + 6x^2 + 12x + 1$

Q20 The temperature (in °C) of a room is given by the formula $C = -20t^3 + 40t^2 - 10$,
where t is the time in hours after a heater was turned on (for $0 \le t \le 2$).

a) What was the temperature of the room when the heater was turned on?

b) What was the rate of temperature change after 30 minutes?

c) After some time, the heater was turned off. The room started to cool immediately.
At what time was the heater switched off?

Scale Drawings

Watch out for those units... there's quite a mixture here —
you'll have to convert some of them before you can go anywhere.

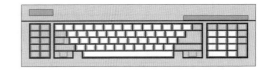

Q1 A rectangular room measures 20 m long and 15 m wide. Work out the measurements for a scale drawing of the room using a scale of 1 cm = 2 m.

Q2 Katie drew a scale drawing of the top of her desk. She used a scale of 1:10. This is her drawing of the computer keyboard. What are its actual dimensions?

Q3

| Cupboards | Oven | Cupboards |

This is a scale drawing of part of Paul's kitchen. Measure the width of the gap for the oven.

The drawing uses a scale of 1 : 60.
Work out the maximum width of oven, in cm, that Paul can buy.

Q4 A rectangular room is 4.8 m long and 3.6 m wide.
a) Make a scale drawing of it using a scale of 1 cm to 120 cm.
b) On your scale drawing mark a window which has an actual length of 2.4 m on one long wall and mark a door, actual width 90 cm, on one shorter wall.

Q5 The scale on this map is 1 cm : 4 km.

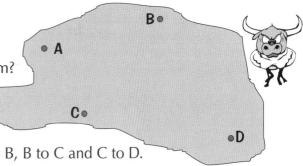

a) Measure the distance from A to B in cm.

b) What is the actual distance from A to B in km?

c) A helicopter flies on a direct route from A to B, B to C and C to D. What is the total distance flown in km?

Q6 Frank has made a scale drawing of his garden to help him plan some improvements. The scale on the drawing is 1 : 70.

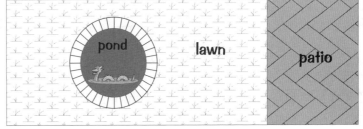

a) Frank wants to put up a fence along the three outside edges of the lawn. How many metres of fencing does he need to buy?

b) What is the actual area of Frank's patio in m?

If the scale doesn't say what units it's in, it just means that both sides of the ratio are the same units — so <u>1 : 1000</u> would mean <u>1 cm : 1000 cm.</u>

Symmetry

Two types of symmetry here — but don't worry, I reckon
their names pretty much give the game away.

There are TWO types of symmetry to learn:	
1) LINE SYMMETRY	You can draw a mirror line across the object and both sides will fold together exactly.
2) ROTATIONAL SYMMETRY	You can rotate the shape or drawing into different positions that all look exactly the same.

Q1 Draw <u>all</u> the lines of symmetry for each of the following shapes.
(Some shapes may have no lines of symmetry.)

a)   **b)**   **c)**   **d)**   **e)**   **f)**

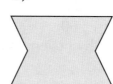

*These questions are a piece of cake if you use
tracing paper — you can use it in the Exam
too, so take some with you or ask for it.*

Q2 What is the <u>order of rotational symmetry</u> for each of the following shapes?

a)   **b)**   **c)**   **d)**

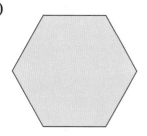
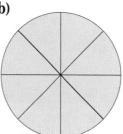
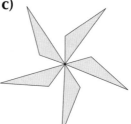
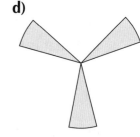

Q3 Mark in the <u>lines of symmetry</u> of the following letters. State the <u>order</u> of rotational
symmetry for each one.

MHVAKSZ

Q4 Draw an example of each of the following shapes. Put in the <u>axes of symmetry</u> and
state the <u>order</u> of rotational symmetry.

a) An equilateral triangle.   **d)** An isosceles trapezium.
b) An isosceles triangle.   **e)** A regular octagon.
c) A rhombus.   **f)** A parallelogram.

Polygons

The one thing they're <u>guaranteed</u> to ask you about is <u>Interior and Exterior Angles</u> —
you'd better get learning those formulas...

> A <u>POLYGON</u> is a many-sided shape. A <u>REGULAR</u> polygon is
> one where <u>ALL THE SIDES AND ANGLES ARE THE SAME</u>.
>
> You need to know these two formulas:
> 1) EXTERIOR ANGLE = 360° ÷ No. of Sides
> 2) INTERIOR ANGLE = 180° – EXTERIOR ANGLE

Q1 What sort of triangles occur in every <u>regular polygon</u> (<u>except</u> a hexagon), when each vertex is joined to the centre by a straight line?

Q2 Sketch a regular hexagon and draw in all its lines of symmetry.
State the order of <u>rotational</u> symmetry.

Q3 In each of the pentagons below, all the sides are of equal length, two of the angles are 90° and the other interior angles are m, m, and r degrees.

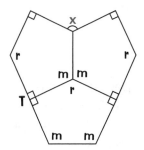

   a) Explain in <u>two</u> different ways why 2m + r = 360°.
   b) What is the size of angle x?
   c) Copy the diagram and add two more pentagons (by tracing through) so that the point T is completely surrounded and the whole figure forms part of a tessellation. Label all the angles of the new pentagons.

Q4 A square and a regular hexagon are placed adjacent to each other.
   a) What is the size of ∠PQW?
   b) What is the size of ∠PRW?
   c) How many sides has the regular polygon that has ∠PQW as one of its angles?

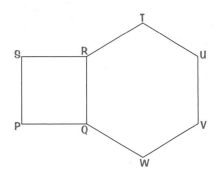

Q5 An <u>irregular pentagon</u> has interior angles of 100°, 104°, 120°.
If the other two angles are equal, what is their size?

Q6 **a)** The <u>sum</u> of the <u>interior</u> angles of a <u>regular</u> 24-sided polygon is 3960°.
Use this to calculate the size of one <u>interior</u> angle.
   b) From your answer to part **a)** calculate one <u>exterior</u> angle and show that the <u>sum</u> of the exterior angles equals 360°.

Polygons

Q7

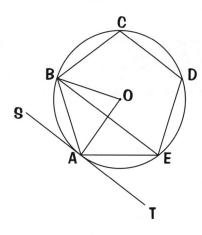

ABCDE is a regular pentagon. It is drawn in a circle with centre O. SAT is a tangent drawn to the circle at A.

a) Calculate the size of angle BOA.

b) Find the size of angle OBA.

c) Write down the size of angle:

    i) SAO

    ii) BAS.

d) Hence write down the size of angle BEA, giving a reason for your answer.

Q8 The sum of the interior angles of a regular polygon is 2520°. How many sides does this regular polygon have?

Remember that formula for the sum of interior angles — it comes in handy here.

Q9

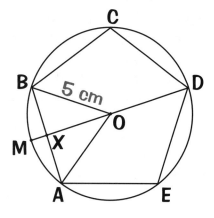

ABCDE is a regular pentagon whose vertices lie on a circle of radius 5 cm, centre O. DOM is an axis of symmetry of the pentagon and cuts the chord AB at X.

a) Calculate the size of angle BOX.

b) Find the length OX. Hence find the distance of M from the chord AB.

*You need to use trigonometry to find **OX** — cos θ = adj / hyp.*

Q10 ABCDEFGH is a regular octagon.

a) Copy the figure and mark on the axis of symmetry which maps H to A.

b) Calculate the size of angle EFC.

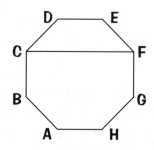

Perimeters and Areas

Q1 Calculate the area and perimeter of the rectangle.

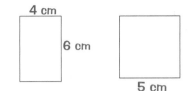

4 cm

6 cm

5 cm

Q2 Calculate the area and perimeter of the square.

Q3 An attachment on a child's toy is made from plastic in the shape of an octagon with a square cut out. A diagram of the attachment is shown on the right. By counting squares or otherwise, find the area of plastic needed to make 4 of these attachments.

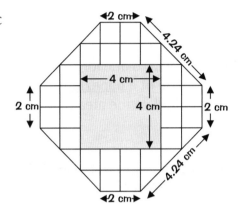

Q4 A rectangular dining room, with a width equal to half its length, needs carpet tiling.
  a) Calculate the area of the floor, if its width is 12 m.
  b) If carpet tiles are 50 cm by 50 cm squares, calculate how many tiles will be required.
  c) If carpet tiles cost £4.99 per m², calculate the cost of tiling the dining room.

Q5 Using π = 3.14, find:
  a) The area of a circle with radius = 6.12 m. Give your answer to 3 d.p.
  b) The circumference of a circle with radius = 7.2 m. Give your answer to 2 s.f.
  c) The circumference of a circle with diameter = 14.8 m. Give your answer to 1 d.p.
  d) The area of a circle with diameter = 4.246 cm. Give answer your to 3 d.p.

Q6 Josh is making a cube-shaped bean bag out of material for his textiles coursework. To make each side of the cube he needs a square of material with edges of length 60 cm. How many square metres of material will Josh need?

Q7 Find the area and the perimeter of each of the shapes drawn here. Use π = 3.14.

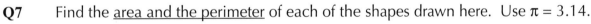

a)

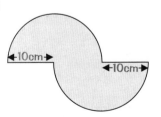

10cm

10cm

b)

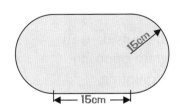

15cm

15cm

c)

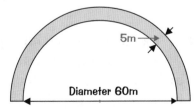

5m

Diameter 60m

Q8 Natasha is training for a marathon by jogging around the outside of a square field of area 9000 m². One evening, Natasha completed 11 laps of the field. How far did she run? Give your answer to the nearest 100 m.

SECTION FIVE — SHAPES, VECTORS AND TRANSFORMATIONS

Perimeters and Areas

Q9 A lawn is to be made 48 m². If its width is 5 m, how long is it? How many rolls of turf 50 cm wide and 11 m long should be ordered to grass this area?

Q10 This parallelogram has an area of 4773 mm². How long is its <u>base</u>?

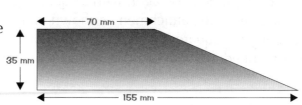

Q11 A metal blade for a craft knife is the shape of a <u>trapezium</u>, as shown. Calculate the area of the metal.

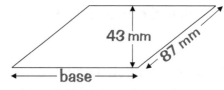

If you can't remember the formula for the area of a trapezium, you can always split the shape into a rectangle and a triangle.

Q12 Jon is making a metal bracket as part of his technology project. The bracket is stamped out of sheet metal in a 2-phase process:
1st: The <u>outer triangle</u>, measuring 14.4 cm by 10 cm, is stamped out.
2nd: A smaller <u>inner triangle</u> measuring 5.76 cm by 4 cm is stamped out of the larger triangle.
The bracket should be made from no more than 50 cm² of sheet metal if the fixing is to support its weight. Will the fixing take the weight of Jon's bracket?

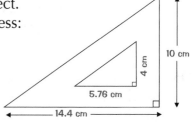

Q13

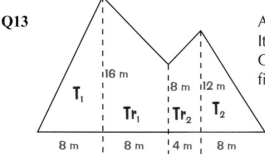

A modern glass sculpture is to be erected. It is made from glass in the shape of two mountain peaks. Calculate each <u>separate</u> area and hence find the <u>total</u> area of glass required.

Q14 You have been asked to paint the outside wall of a building shown in the diagram opposite.
a) Find the area of wall that needs painting.
b) A 1 litre tin of paint will cover 13 m². How many 1 litre tins are needed to give the wall two coats of paint?
c) The wall is also going to have a tiled border around the edge. Calculate the length of the edge of the wall to be tiled.

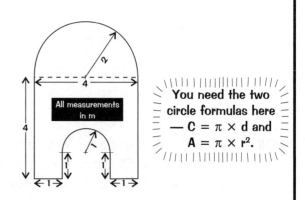

You need the two circle formulas here — C = π × d and A = π × r².

Perimeters and Areas

Q15   A fighter aircraft's wing is shown on the right.
Calculate its <u>area</u>, and its <u>perimeter</u>.

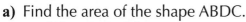

Two lots of Pythagoras are needed
to find the length of the third side.

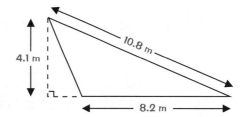

Q16   A simple tent is to be made in the shape of a triangular
prism. The dimensions are shown in the diagram.
a) The two end faces are isosceles triangles.
Find their areas.
b) The two sides and ground sheet are rectangles.
Find their areas.
c) How much material is required to make
this tent?

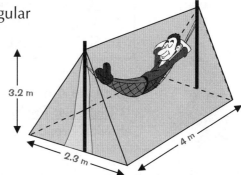

Q17   Calculate the area of a <u>rhombus</u> with diagonals 7 km and 11 km.

Q18   A plastic strip is made in the shape shown.
The curves AC and BD are both arcs of
circles with centre O. The larger circle has
radius 30 mm and the smaller circle has
radius 20 mm. The shaded ends of the shape
are both semicircles.

a) Find the area of the shape ABDC.
b) Find the area of the two semicircular ends.
Hence write down the area of the complete shape.

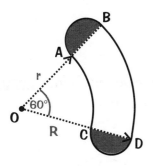

Suppose the radius of the arc AC
is now r and that of BD is R.
c) Write down a formula for the area of the sector OBD
in terms of R.
d) Write down an expression for the area of the shape
ABDC in terms of r and R.
e) Hence write down an expression for the area of the
complete shape.

Q19
**Side
View**

A washing powder ball looks from the side like a
circle with the shaded area removed. The circle has
radius 5 cm and the angle AOB = 80°.
a) Find the area of the sector OAB.
b) Find the area of triangle AOB and
hence the area of the shaded area.

The formula you
need for part b) is
area = ½absin(c).

Solids and Nets

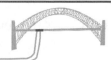

Before you go any further — make sure you know these 3 facts...

Surface Area and Nets

1) <u>SURFACE AREA</u> only applies to solid 3D objects. It's the <u>TOTAL AREA</u> of all the <u>OUTER SURFACES</u> added together.
2) A <u>NET</u> is just a <u>SOLID SHAPE</u> folded out <u>FLAT</u>.
3) SURFACE AREA OF SOLID = AREA OF NET.

There are 4 nets that you need to know inside out... so to speak:
1) <u>Triangular Prism</u>, 2) <u>Cube</u>, 3) <u>Cuboid</u>, 4) <u>Pyramid</u>. I reckon you shouldn't read any further till you're 100% happy with them.

Q1 The net shown will fold to make a cube.
Only one flap is shown. <u>Copy</u> the diagram.

a) Put an X in each corner that touches Y when the cube is made up.
b) Put an F where the flap will join one face to another when the cube is made up.
c) Put on the other flaps necessary to glue the cube together.

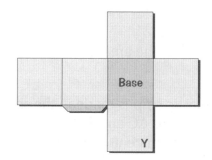

Q2 Draw an <u>accurate</u> net that would fold to make the 3D cuboid shown (diagram is not full size).
It is not necessary to include flaps.

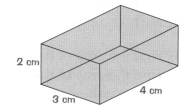

Q3 Draw a <u>full size net</u> (without flaps) of a square-based pyramid whose base has sides of length 3 cm.

Q4 Julie is designing new packaging boxes for her home-made jewellery. Draw <u>accurately</u> the net of a triangular-based pyramid, with sufficient flaps to glue it together.

Q5 a) What shape is the <u>base</u> of the cuboid shown opposite?
b) Which edges are the same length as DE?
c) Which lengths equal CE?
d) Which lengths equal the diagonal DG?
e) How many vertices does the cuboid have?

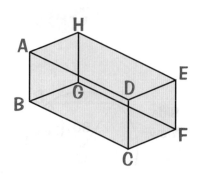

Q6 Draw a <u>circular cone</u>.
a) How many vertices does it have?
b) How many edges?

Solids and Nets

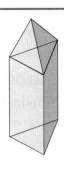

Q7 An equilateral triangular prism has a triangular-based pyramid
placed on top of it, as shown. For this <u>combined</u> solid:
  a) How many edges does it have?
  b) How many vertices?
  c) How many faces?

Q8

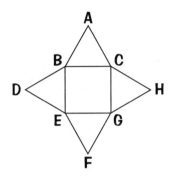

The diagram shows the net of a solid in which ABC
is an equilateral triangle and BCGE is a square.
  a) Which points will coincide with A when the net is
  folded up to make the solid?
  b) Describe the symmetry of the net.
  c) How many faces, edges and vertices does it have
  when in solid form?

Q9 The diagram shows the net of a cube of edge 8 cm.

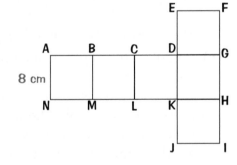

  a) Which point coincides with M when the net is
  folded to make the cube?
  b) Find the area of the face DGHK.
  c) What is the total surface area of the cube?

Q10

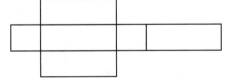

This diagram shows a net for a
rectangular box with a lid. For the
same box sketch a different net.

Q11 Which of these two nets will
form a pyramid on a triangular
base with all four faces
equilateral triangles?

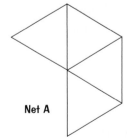

Net A

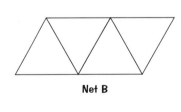

Net B

Q12

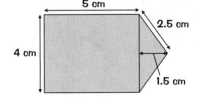

The diagram shows part of the net of a triangular prism.
  a) Copy and complete the net.
  It is not necessary to include flaps.
  b) What is the surface area of the prism?

Surface Area and Volume

Make sure you can use those <u>formulas</u> — the ones below might be useful on these pages.

Cylinder:
Curved surface
area = πr²h
Volume = 2πrh

Sphere:
Surface area = 4πr²
Volume = $\frac{4}{3}$πr³

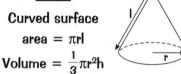

Cone:
Curved surface
area = πrl
Volume = $\frac{1}{3}$πr²h

Q1 Joe buys a polythene tunnel to protect his plants from frost. It has a semicircular diameter of 70 cm and a length of 3 m.
a) Find the cross-sectional area.
b) Hence find the volume of the tunnel.

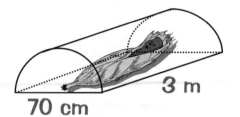

3 m

70 cm

Q2 I am planning to build a circular pond in my garden surrounded by a ring shaped paved area.
The pond will be 50 cm deep and filled with water.
a) Calculate the approximate cost of paving the area around the pond with slabs costing £16 per m². Give your answer to the nearest £10.
b) I need to add 15 ml of liquid pond treatment for every m³ of water in the pond. Find the volume of treatment I will need to add to the pond. Give your answer to the nearest ml.

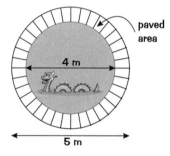

paved area

4 m

5 m

Q3 A solid metal cube, each of whose sides is 10 cm long, is melted down and made into a solid cylinder 10 cm high.
a) What is the radius of this cylinder?
b) Find the surface area of the cylinder.

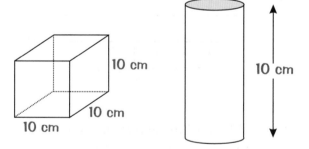

10 cm

10 cm

10 cm

10 cm

Q4 A tin mug has the dimensions shown.
a) What is the greatest volume of milk the mug can hold?
b) In fact, 600 cm³ of milk is poured in. How high will it go up the mug?

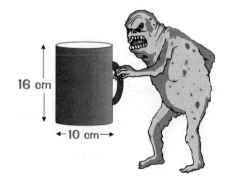

16 cm

←10 cm→

SECTION FIVE — SHAPES, VECTORS AND TRANSFORMATIONS

Surface Area and Volume

Q5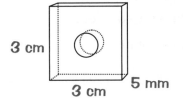

3 cm

3 cm   5 mm

A nut has the cross-section illustrated. The circular hole has a diameter of 1.4 cm and the nut is 5 mm thick. Find the volume of the nut in cm³.

(Units...)

Q6 Water is flowing into each of these containers at a constant rate. For each container, sketch the graph of the depth of water against time.

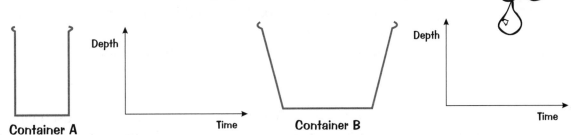

Depth

Container A   Time

Depth

Container B   Time

Q7 Steve has bought a pair of speaker stands. The base of each stand is a hollow prism with the dimensions shown. A hollow tube of diameter 4 cm and height 110 cm screws into the top of each base to form the stand.

Steve is filling the stands with sand to improve stability. Find the volume of sand Steve needs to use to fill both stands (the bases <u>and</u> the tubes). Give your answer in litres to 2 d.p.

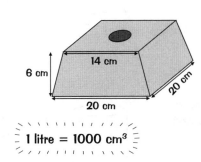

14 cm

6 cm

20 cm   20 cm

1 litre = 1000 cm³

Q8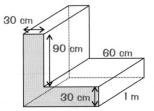

30 cm

90 cm   60 cm

30 cm   1 m

Jill buys a bookshelf with the dimensions shown in the diagram.

a) Find the cross-sectional area.

b) Find the volume of the bookshelf in m³.

Q9 Bill has a greenhouse with dimensions as shown. The roof is made up of eight panels of equal size.

A storm breaks all of the glass in the shaded area on the diagram.

Calculate the area of glass which Bill must buy to repair his greenhouse.

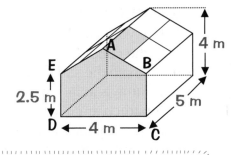

A   4 m

E   B

2.5 m   5 m

D ← 4 m → C

Look for a right-angled triangle to calculate AB.

Surface Area and Volume

Q10

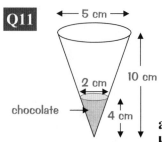

2.6 cm

1.8 cm

1.2 cm

An egg timer is symmetrical and consists of hemispheres, cylinders and cones joined together as shown to the left.

a) Calculate the volume of sand in the upper container.

> You need to find three volumes and add them together.

Sand runs into the bottom container at a constant rate of 0.05 cm³ per second. At the end of a certain time period the sand has fallen through into the bottom container as shown to the right.

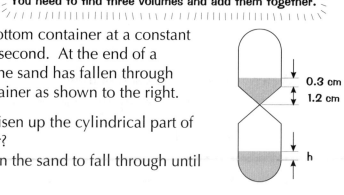

0.3 cm

1.2 cm

h

b) How high (*h*) has it risen up the cylindrical part of the bottom container?

c) How long has it taken the sand to fall through until it is at this height?

Q11

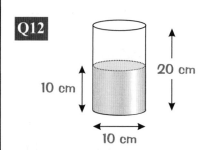

5 cm

10 cm

2 cm

10 cm

chocolate

4 cm

To make a 'Bandito's Barnetto', an ice-cream cone is used which is 10 cm deep and has a base diameter of 5 cm. The tip of the cone is filled 4 cm deep with solid chocolate as shown. The rest of the cone is filled with ice cream and a hemisphere of ice cream is mounted on top so that the base of the hemisphere coincides with the base of the cone.

a) Calculate the volume of ice cream required for just one Barnetto.

b) Calculate the outer surface area of the cone.

Q12

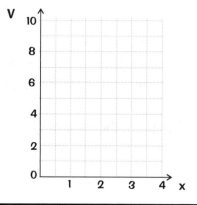

20 cm

10 cm

10 cm

Mike and Shelly are doing an experiment to find the radius of a marble. They fill a cylindrical container of diameter 10 cm and height 20 cm with water to a depth of 10 cm. 200 identical marbles are now submerged in the water. The depth increases to 14.5 cm. Calculate the radius of one marble.

> The volume increase is a cylinder and you're told the height.

Q13 A cuboid has a height of *x* m, a width of (3 − *x*) m and a length of (5 − *x*) m.

a) Write down an expression for the volume of the cuboid.

b) Complete the table of values using your expression for the volume of the cuboid.

x	0	1	2	3
V			6	

c) Draw a graph of V against *x* for 0 ≤ *x* ≤ 3.

d) Use your graph to estimate the maximum volume of the cuboid.

e) Estimate the surface area of the cuboid when the volume is at its maximum.

f) A particular cuboid has a volume of 6 m³. By using your graph to find the two possible values of *x*, estimate the maximum total surface area of the cuboid for this volume.

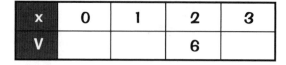

V

10

8

6

4

2

0

1 2 3 4 x

Vectors

If you've got some squared or graph paper handy, it just might
be useful for the first few questions on this page...

Q1 ABCDE is a pentagon.

$$\vec{AB} = \begin{pmatrix} 3 \\ 3 \end{pmatrix} \quad \vec{AC} = \begin{pmatrix} 2 \\ 6 \end{pmatrix} \quad \vec{AD} = \begin{pmatrix} -2 \\ 6 \end{pmatrix} \quad \vec{AE} = \begin{pmatrix} -3 \\ 2 \end{pmatrix}$$

a) Draw this pentagon accurately.

b) Write down the vectors:

   i) $\vec{DE}$ ii) $\vec{DC}$ iii) $\vec{EC}$

c) What sort of triangle is $\triangle$ACD?

Q2 ABC is a triangle.

$$\vec{AB} = \begin{pmatrix} 4 \\ 0 \end{pmatrix} \quad \vec{BC} = \begin{pmatrix} 0 \\ 3 \end{pmatrix}$$

a) Draw this triangle accurately.

b) Find $|\vec{AC}|$.

Q3 $p = \begin{pmatrix} 2 \\ 3 \end{pmatrix}, q = \begin{pmatrix} 0 \\ -2 \end{pmatrix}, r = \begin{pmatrix} 3 \\ -1 \end{pmatrix}, s = \begin{pmatrix} -1 \\ -2 \end{pmatrix}$

Calculate then draw:

a) $p + q$ c) $2r$ e) $2p - 2s$ g) $2r - q$ i) $p + 2s$

b) $p - q$ d) $s + p$ f) $3q + s$ h) $\frac{1}{2}q + 2r$ j) $q - 2r$

Q4 Find the magnitude of the following vectors:

a) $\begin{pmatrix} 1 \\ 0 \end{pmatrix}$ c) $\begin{pmatrix} 0 \\ -1 \end{pmatrix}$ e) $\begin{pmatrix} 1 \\ 6 \end{pmatrix}$ g) $\begin{pmatrix} 5 \\ 7 \end{pmatrix}$ i) $\begin{pmatrix} -8 \\ 5 \end{pmatrix}$

b) $\begin{pmatrix} 3 \\ 2 \end{pmatrix}$ d) $\begin{pmatrix} -2 \\ 3 \end{pmatrix}$ f) $\begin{pmatrix} 4 \\ -3 \end{pmatrix}$ h) $\begin{pmatrix} 6 \\ 6 \end{pmatrix}$ j) $\begin{pmatrix} -10 \\ -5 \end{pmatrix}$

Q5 $e = \begin{pmatrix} 5 \\ 2 \end{pmatrix}, f = \begin{pmatrix} -2 \\ 1 \end{pmatrix}, g = \begin{pmatrix} 7 \\ -3 \end{pmatrix}, h = \begin{pmatrix} -3 \\ -4 \end{pmatrix}$

Find:

a) $e + f$ c) $f + g$ e) $e + h$

b) $|e + f|$ d) $|f + g|$ f) $|e + h|$

SECTION FIVE — SHAPES, VECTORS AND TRANSFORMATIONS

Vectors

Q6

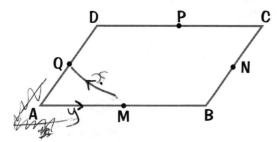

ABCD is a parallelogram. M, N, P and Q are the mid-points of the sides, as shown.
$\overrightarrow{MQ} = x$ and $\overrightarrow{AM} = y$.

Express in terms of x and y:

a) $\overrightarrow{AB}$ $2y$

b) $\overrightarrow{AQ}$

c) $\overrightarrow{NB}$

d) $\overrightarrow{BC}$

e) $\overrightarrow{AC}$

f) $\overrightarrow{BD}$

Q7 In the diagram on the right, EB and AC are perpendicular. ABCE is a parallelogram. ∠EDC is a right angle.

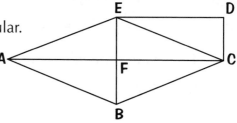

a) Name a vector equal to:

i) $\overrightarrow{FC}$

ii) $\overrightarrow{FB}$

iii) $\overrightarrow{BC}$

iv) $\overrightarrow{CE}$

v) $2\overrightarrow{CD}$

vi) $\overrightarrow{AE} + \overrightarrow{EC}$

vii) $\overrightarrow{EF} - \overrightarrow{CF}$

viii) $\overrightarrow{ED} + \overrightarrow{DC} + \overrightarrow{CB}$

b) If AC = 16 cm and EB = 6 cm:

i) what is the area of ABCE?

ii) what is the area of ABCDE?

Q8 ABC is a triangle.

P is the point on BA such that BA = 2PA.

Q is the point on BC such that BC = 2BQ.

$\overrightarrow{BQ} = a$, $\overrightarrow{PA} = b$.

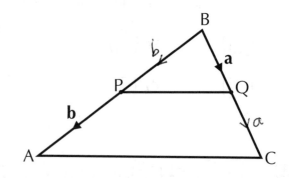

a) Express in terms of **a** and **b**:

i) $\overrightarrow{BC}$ $2a$

ii) $\overrightarrow{CP}$ $-2a + b$

iii) $\overrightarrow{PQ}$ $a - b$

b) Prove that $\overrightarrow{PQ}$ is parallel to $\overrightarrow{AC}$.

The Four Transformations

Only 4 of these to learn... and good old TERRY's always around to help if you need him.

Q1 A is the point (4, 3), B is (4, 1) and
C is (5, 1).

  a) Using a scale of 1 cm to 1 unit
  draw the axes and mark on it
  the figure given by ABC.

  b) Reflect ABC in the *x*-axis and
  label the image $A_1B_1C_1$.

  c) Reflect $A_1B_1C_1$ in the *y*-axis and
  label the image $A_2B_2C_2$.

  d) Describe fully the single transformation
  which would map ABC onto $A_2B_2C_2$.

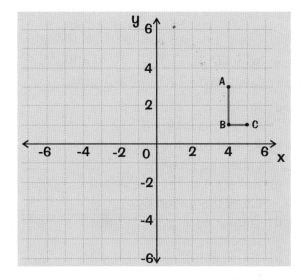

Q2 Copy the axes using a scale of 1 cm to
1 unit. Mark on the axes a quadrilateral
Q with corners (-2, 1), (-3, 1), (-3, 3)
and (-2, 2).

  a) Rotate Q clockwise through 90°
  about the point (-1, 2). Label the
  image R.

  b) Rotate R clockwise through 90°
  about the point (0, 1). Label the
  image S.

  c) Describe fully the rotation that
  maps Q to S.

  d) Rotate Q through 180° about the
  point (-½, -1). Label the image T.

  e) Rotate Q anticlockwise through 90°
  about the point (-1, -1). Label the
  image U.

  f) Describe fully the rotation that sends U to T.

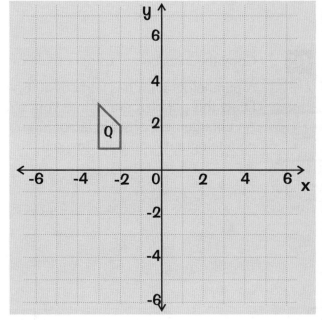

Q3 Draw axes with *x* and *y* running from 0 to 12 with a scale of 1 cm to 1 unit.
O is the origin. $\overrightarrow{OP} = \begin{pmatrix} 4 \\ 2 \end{pmatrix}$, $\overrightarrow{PQ} = \begin{pmatrix} -1 \\ 2 \end{pmatrix}$, and $\overrightarrow{QR} = 2\overrightarrow{OP}$.

  a) Mark P, Q and R on your axes.

  b) Translate R by $\overrightarrow{QO}$. Label the image T.

  c) Verify that $\overrightarrow{PQ} + \overrightarrow{QR} + \overrightarrow{RT} + \overrightarrow{TP} = O$.

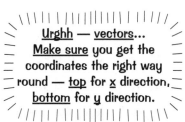

Urghh — vectors...
Make sure you get the
coordinates the right way
round — top for x direction,
bottom for y direction.

SECTION FIVE — SHAPES, VECTORS AND TRANSFORMATIONS

The Four Transformations

Move each point separately — then check your shape hasn't
done anything unexpected while you weren't looking.

Q4 Copy the axes and mark on triangle A
with corners (-1, 2), (0, 4) and (-2, 4).
Use a scale of 1 cm to 1 unit.

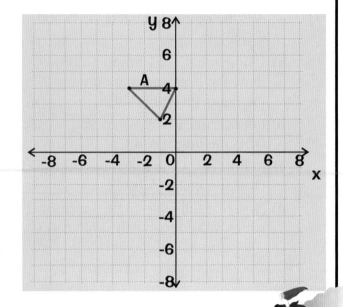

a) Reflect A in the line $y = -x$.
Label this image B.

b) Reflect A in the line $x = 1$.
Label the image C.

c) Reflect A in the line $y = -1$.
Label the image D.

d) Translate triangle D with the vector $\begin{pmatrix} 4 \\ 2 \end{pmatrix}$.
Label this image E.

e) Translate triangle C with the vector $\begin{pmatrix} 3 \\ -3 \end{pmatrix}$.
Label this image F.

f) Describe fully the transformation that
sends C to E.

Q5 Copy the axes below using a scale of 1 cm to 1 unit.

A parallelogram A has vertices at (6, 4), (10, 4), (8, 10) and (12, 10).
Draw this parallelogram onto your axes.
An enlargement of scale factor ½ and centre (0, 0) transforms
parallelogram A onto its image B.

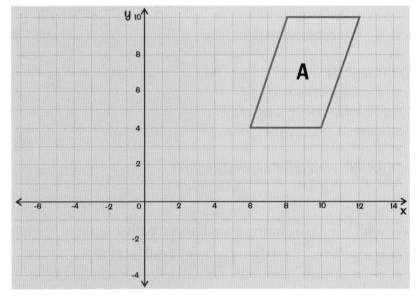

a) Draw this image B on your axes.

b) Translate B by the vector $\begin{pmatrix} -3 \\ -2 \end{pmatrix}$ and label this image C.

c) Calculate the ratio of the area of parallelogram C to the area of parallelogram A.

Congruence, Similarity and Enlargement

Q1 Which pair of triangles are congruent? Explain why.

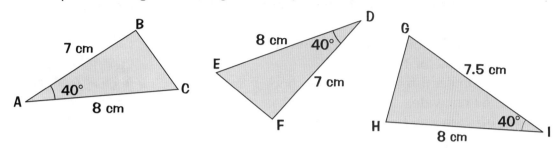

Q2 In the diagram below, BC is parallel to DE.
AB = 12 cm, BD = 8 cm, DE = 25 cm and CE = 10 cm.

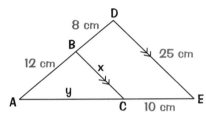

a) Explain why triangles ABC and ADE are similar.
b) Find the lengths of x and y in the diagram.

Q3 Another triangle, congruent to the triangle shown on the
right, must be drawn with vertices at three of the dots.
Show in how many different ways this can be done.

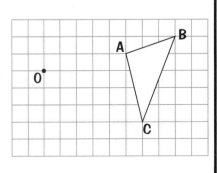

Q4 A boy made a symmetrical framework with metal rods as shown. Lengths AB = BC,
ST = TC and AP = PQ. Angle BVC = 90° and length BV = 9 cm.

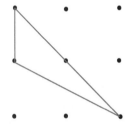

a) Find two triangles which are similar to
triangle ABC.
b) Calculate the length of AP. Hence write
down the length of PT.
c) Calculate the area of triangle ABC.
d) Find the area of triangle APQ. Give your
answer correct to 3 significant figures.
e) Hence write down the area of PQBST correct to 2 significant figures.

Q5 Copy the diagram on the right onto squared paper.

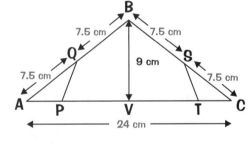

a) Draw an enlargement of the triangle ABC of scale factor 2.
Use the point O as the centre of enlargement and label the
image $A_1B_1C_1$.
b) Rotate triangle ABC through 180° about the point O.
Label the image $A_2B_2C_2$.
c) Which image is congruent to triangle ABC?

Congruence, Similarity and Enlargement

**Don't forget that when you're enlarging areas and volumes,
there's a bigger scale factor — that one catches everyone out.**

Q6 Sharon has a fish tank which is 42 cm wide
and has a volume of 30 litres.
She sees a similar fish tank in the pet shop
which is 63 cm wide.

What is the volume of the larger fish tank
to the nearest litre?

Q7 A cylindrical bottle can hold 1 litre of oil. A second cylindrical bottle has
twice the radius but the same height. It also contains oil.
a) Explain why these bottles are not similar.
b) How much oil can the larger bottle hold?

Q8 For a graphics project, Eliza makes a model of a chocolate
box in the shape of a cuboid 5 cm long, 2 cm wide and
3 cm high.
a) Calculate the area of material needed to make the model
(assuming no flaps are required for glueing).
b) Eliza decides that the full size packaging will be similar to
the model, but enlarged by a scale factor of 4. Calculate
the area of material Eliza needs to make a full-size box.

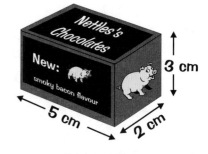

Q9 On a holiday near the sea, children built a sandcastle in the shape of a cone.
The radius of the base is 100 cm and the height is 100 cm.

a) What is the volume of the sandcastle in m³ correct to
3 significant figures?
The children now remove the
top portion to make a similar
cone but only 50 cm in height.
b) State the radius of the base of this
smaller cone.
c) State the ratio of the volume of the small
cone to the volume of the original cone.
d) Calculate the volume of the small cone in m³ correct to
3 significant figures.
e) Hence write down the ratio of the volume of the portion left of the original cone to the
smaller cone in the form n:1.

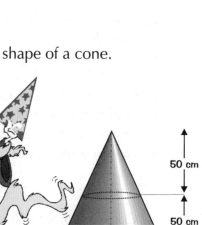

Constructions

Work through these questions bit by bit, and remember...

BISECTOR — a line splitting an angle or line exactly in two.

Q1 **a)** Construct a triangle ABC with AB = 4 cm, BC = 5 cm, AC = 3 cm.

b) Construct the perpendicular bisector of AB and where this line meets BC, label the new point D.

Q2 Construct triangle PQR accurately with length PQ = 10.5 cm, angle PQR = 95° and angle RPQ = 32°.

a) Construct the perpendicular bisector of the line PR. Draw in point A where the bisector crosses the line PQ.

b) Bisect angle PRQ. Draw in point B where the bisector crosses the line PQ. Measure the length BA.

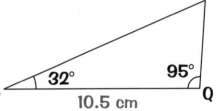

Q3 Use a ruler and compasses to construct square ABCD accurately with length AB = 6.5 cm.

a) Construct the bisectors of angles BAD and ADC. Mark the point O where the 2 bisectors cross.

b) Bisect the angle OAD.

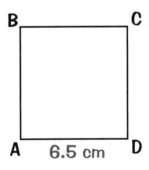

Q4 Construct triangle PQR with length PQ = QR = 11.5 cm and angle PQR = 38°.

a) Construct the bisectors of angles QPR and QRP. Mark the point O where the 2 bisectors cross.

b) With centre O draw the circle which just touches the sides PQ, PR and QR of the triangle. What is the radius of this circle?

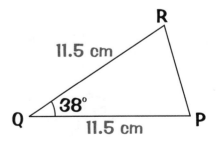

Angle Geometry

Here are some angle rules then — just the 7 for now. You can't get away without knowing these, I'm afraid, so get learning.

1) Angles in a triangle <u>add up to 180°</u>

2) Angles in a 4-sided shape <u>add up to 360°</u>

3) Angles round a point <u>add up to 360°</u>

4) When a line crosses <u>TWO PARALLEL LINES</u>, the two bunches of angles are the same

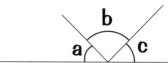

5) Angles on a straight line <u>add up to 180°</u>

6) <u>ISOSCELES TRIANGLES</u> have two sides the same and two angles the same

7) <u>EXTERIOR</u> angle of a triangle = sum of opposite <u>INTERIOR</u> angles.

d = a + b

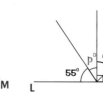

For the following diagrams, find the <u>lettered</u> angles.   LM is a straight line.

Q1 a)   **b)**   **c)**   **d)**

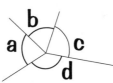

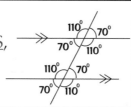

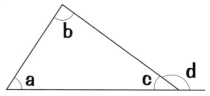

Q2 a)   **b)**   **c)**   **d)**

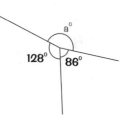

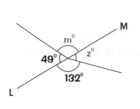

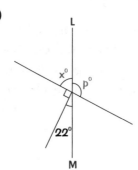

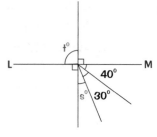

Angle Geometry

This page is a bit dull — just lots of boring angles... still, that's geometry for you. Oh and by the way, you've got to work the angles out — don't try and sneakily measure them, they're probably drawn wrong anyway...

For the following diagrams, find the <u>lettered</u> angles. LM is a straight line.

Q3 **a)**   **b)**   **c)**   **d)**

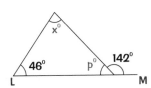 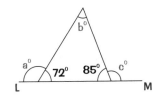 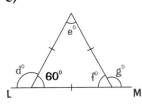 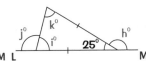

Q4 **a)**   **b)**   **c)**

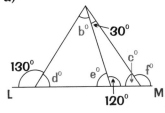 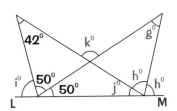 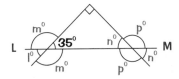

\\\\\\\\\\\\\\\\\\\\\\\\\\\\\\\
Keep an eye out for parallel lines — they'll help no end...
as long as you can remember the angle rules, of course.
/////////////////////////////

Q5 **a)**   **b)**   **c)**

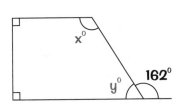 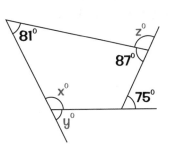 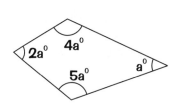

Q6 **a)**   **b)**   **c)**

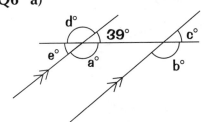 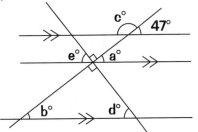 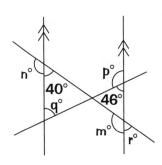

Circle Geometry

Q1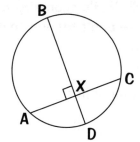

A, B, C and D are points on the circumference of a circle of radius 9 m. The chords AC and BD meet at point X, at an angle of 90°. If AC = 13 m and AX = 6.5 m, what is the length of BD? Explain your answer.

Q2 A, B and C are points on the circumference of a circle with centre O. BD and CD are tangents of the circle.

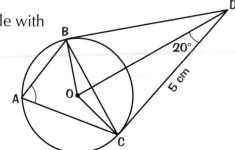

a) State the length BD.
b) Calculate the size of angle COD.
c) State the size of angle COB.

Q3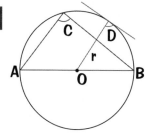

The circle in the diagram to the left contains a triangle with points (A and B) at both ends of a diameter and angle C to the edge of the circle. A tangent has been drawn which makes angle D with the radius, r. O is the centre of the circle.
What are the sizes of the angles C and D?

Q4 ABCD is a cyclic quadrilateral with angle BCD = 100°.
EF is a tangent to the circle touching it at A.
Angle DAF = 30°.
Write down the size of angle:
a) BAD
b) EAB.

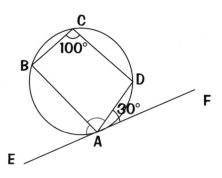

Q5 A, B, C, D and E are points on the circumference of a circle with centre O. Angle BDE = 53°. The line AF is a tangent to the circle, touching it at A.
Angle EAF = 32°. Find:
a) angle BOE
b) angle ACE.

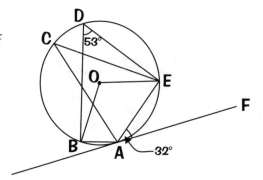

Circle Geometry

Q6 ABCD is a cyclic quadrilateral and the tangent to the circle at A makes an angle of 70° with the side AD. Angle BCA = 30°. Write down, giving a reason, the size of:

a) angle ACD

b) angle BAD.

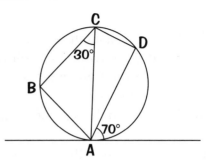

Q7

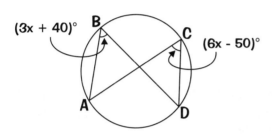

A, B, C and D are points on the circumference of a circle. Angle ABD = $(3x + 40)°$ and angle ACD = $(6x - 50)°$.

a) Give a reason why angle ABD and angle ACD are the same.

b) Form an equation in x and by solving it, find the size of angle ABD.

Q8 O is the centre of a circle and AB is a chord. The length OA = 5 cm and angle OAB = 20°. Find the length of the chord AB.

One way to do this is to work out angle AOB and use the sine rule.

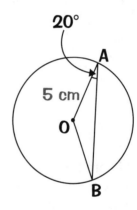

Q9

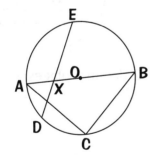

A, B, C, D and E are points on the circumference of a circle with centre O. X is the point at which AB and DE intersect.

a) AC = BC and the area of triangle ABC is 64 cm². What is the length of AB?

b) BX = 3AX, and DX = 6 cm. Find the lengths of EX and DE.

Q10 A, B, C and D are points on the circumference of a circle. O is the centre of the circle and angle AOD = 140°. Write down:

a) angle ABD

b) angle ABC

c) angle DBC.

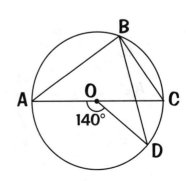

Circle Geometry

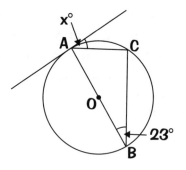

Q11 A tangent of a circle is drawn, touching it at A.
C and B are two other points on the circumference
and AOB is a diameter. O is the centre of the circle.
Angle ABC is 23°.

   a) Write down the size of angle ACB, giving a reason
   for your answer.

   b) Find the size of the angle marked x° in the diagram.

Q12

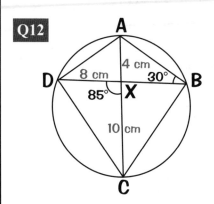

ABCD is a cyclic quadrilateral. The lines AC and BD
intersect at X. Lengths AX = 4 cm, DX = 8 cm and
XC = 10 cm. Angles DXC = 85° and ABD = 30°.

   a) Show that triangles DXC and AXB are similar.

   b) Find the length of XB.

   c) Write down the size of angle BDC.

Q13 B, C and D are three points on the circumference
of a circle with BD as a diameter. O is the centre
of the circle and ADC is a straight line.
AB = 10 cm and BC = 3 cm.

   a) Write down the size of angle ACB,
   giving a reason for your answer.

   b) Show that AC is 9.54 cm correct to 2 decimal places.

   c) If AD = 5 cm, find the length of the diameter DOB correct to 2 decimal places.

Q14

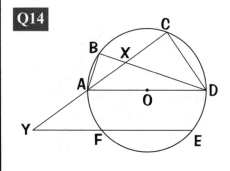

A, B, C, D, E and F are points on the circumference of
a circle. O is the centre of the circle. X is the point at
which AC and BD intersect. AOD, CAY and EFY are all
straight lines.

   a) Write down the size of angles ABD and ACD, giving a
   reason for your answer.

   b) AX = 3 cm, XC = 6.5 cm and XD = 5 cm. Calculate BX.

   c) YE = 6 cm and YA = 2.5 cm. Calculate YF.

Pythagoras and Bearings

Don't try and do it all in your head — you've got to label the sides
or you're bound to mess it up. Go on, get your pen out...

Q1 Find the length of the hypotenuse in each of the following triangles.

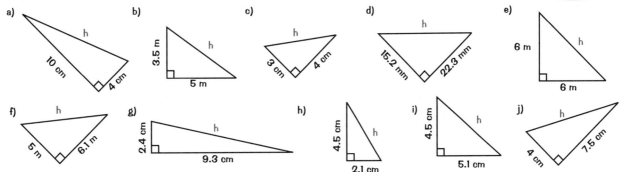

Q2 Find the length of the shorter side in each of the following triangles.

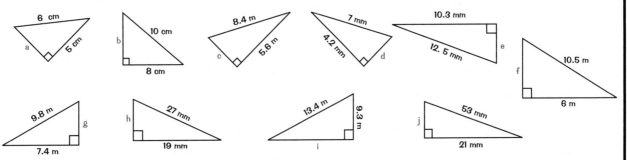

Q3 Find the unknown length in each of the following triangles.

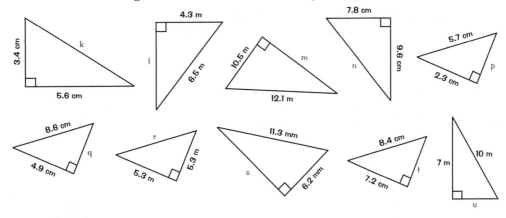

Q4 Find the bearings required in these diagrams.

It's easy to get lost if you don't follow
the easy rule: always measure
bearings from the <u>north line</u>.

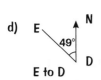
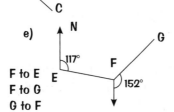
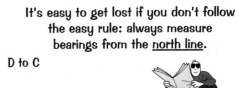
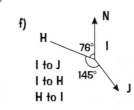

a) $65°$ N B B to A A

b) N $130°$ C to B B C

c) N C $215°$ D to C D

d) E N $49°$ D E to D

e) N $117°$ G F $152°$ F to E E F to G G to F

f) N H $76°$ I I to J $145°$ I to H J H to I

Pythagoras and Bearings

Q5 A window cleaner wants to clean the upstairs windows of an office. To meet safety regulations, his 10 m long ladder needs to be angled so that the bottom of the ladder is at least 2.6 m away from the wall. What is the maximum height that the top of the ladder can reach when used safely? Give your answer to 1 decimal place.

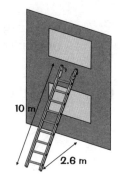

Q6 A rectangular field is 250 m by 190 m. How far is it across diagonally?

Q7 a) Calculate the lengths WY and ZY.
b) What is the total distance WXYZW?
c) What is the area of quadrilateral WXYZ?

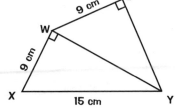

Q8 A plane flies due east for 153 km then turns and flies due north for 116 km. How far is it now from where it started?

Q9 A coastguard spots a boat on a bearing of 040° and at a distance of 350 m. He can also see a tree due east of him. The tree is due south of the boat.
a) Draw a scale diagram and measure accurately the distances from the:
  i) boat to the tree
  ii) coastguard to the tree
b) Check by Pythagoras to see if your answers are reasonable.

> **Top tip**
> The word "<u>from</u>" is the most important word in a bearings question, so look out for it — it tells you where to start <u>from</u>.

Q10 Four towns W, X, Y and Z are situated as follows:
W is 90 km north of X, Y is on a bearing 175° and 165 km from X, X is on a bearing 129° and 123 km from Z. Draw an accurate scale diagram to represent the situation.
From your drawing measure the distances:
a) WZ   **b)** WY   **c)** ZY.
Measure the bearings:
d) Y from Z   **e)** W from Z   **f)** Y from W.

Q11 A walker travels 1200 m on a bearing of 165° and then another 1500 m on a bearing of 210°. By accurate measurement, find how far she is now from her starting point. What bearing must she walk on to return to base?

Q12 A fishing boat travels at 12 km/h for an hour due north. It then turns due west and travels at 7 km/h for an hour. How far is it from its starting point now? What bearing must it travel on to return to base?

Trigonometry

Before you start a trigonometry question, write down the ratios, using
SOH CAH TOA (<u>Sockatoa</u>!) — it'll help you pick your formula.

Q1 Calculate the tan, sin and cos of each of these angles:
   a) 17°   **b)** 83°   **c)** 5°   **d)** 28°   **e)** 45°.

Q2 Use the tangent ratio to find the unknowns:

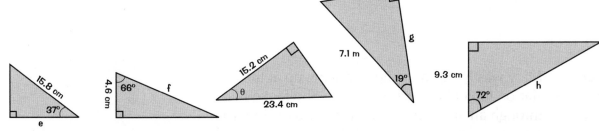

Q3 Use the cosine ratio to find the unknowns:

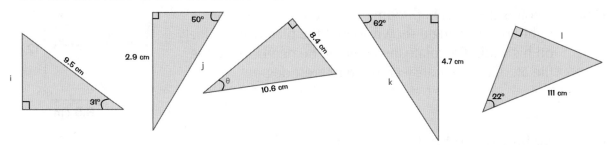

Q4 Use the sine ratio to find the unknowns:

Q5 Find the unknowns using the appropriate ratios:

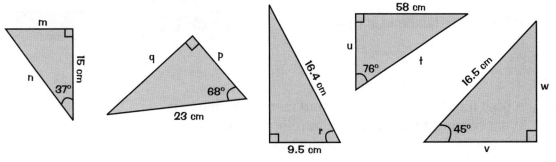

Trigonometry

Q6 A right-angled triangle has sides measuring 30 m, 40 m and 50 m.
   a) Draw a rough sketch of the triangle, clearly labelling the hypotenuse.
   b) Calculate the size of the smallest angle.

Make sure you've got the hang of the inverse SIN, COS and TAN functions on your calc... and check it's in DEG mode or you'll get nowhere fast.

Q7 The points P(1, 2), Q(4, 2) and R(4, -3) when joined together form a right-angled triangle.
   a) Draw a rough sketch of the triangle, labelling the length of each side.
   b) <u>Without measuring</u>, calculate the angle RPQ.
   c) <u>Deduce</u> angle PRQ.

Q8 The points A(1, -2), B(4, -1) and C(1, 3) are the vertices of the triangle ABC.
   a) On graph paper, <u>plot</u> the points A, B and C.
   b) By adding a suitable horizontal line, or otherwise, calculate the angle CAB.
   c) Similarly calculate the angle ACB.
   d) By using the fact that the interior angles of a triangle add up to 180° work out the angle ABC.

Q9 Mary was lying on the floor looking up at the star on top of her Christmas tree. She looked up through an angle of 55° when she was 1.5 m from the base of the tree. How high was the star?

Q10 Geoff is tiling his bathroom. He needs to cut off the right-angled triangle shown so that the tiles will fit nicely on his wall. Calculate the angle, θ, he needs to cut the tile at. Give your answer to the nearest degree.

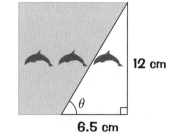

Q11 Mr Brown took his dog for a walk in the park. The dog's lead was 2 m long. The dog ran 0.7 m from the path Mr Brown was walking on.

What angle did the lead make with the path?

Q12 A boat travels 9 km due south and then 7 km due east. What bearing must it travel on to return to base?

SECTION SIX — GEOMETRY

Trigonometry

Q13 This isosceles triangle has a base of 28 cm and a top angle of 54°. Calculate:

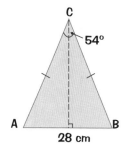

  a) the length of sides AC and BC
  b) the perpendicular height to C
  c) the area of the triangle.

Q14 An isosceles triangle has two equal sides of 7 cm and an angle between them of 65°. Calculate the area of the triangle.

Q15 In this parallelogram the diagonal CB is at right angles to AC. AB is 9.5 cm and ∠CAB is 60°. Calculate:

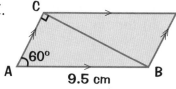

  a) CB   **b)** BD   **c)** the area of the parallelogram.

Q16 This rhombus WXYZ has base of 15 cm and diagonal WY of 28 cm. Calculate the:

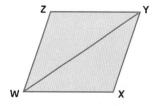

  a) length of diagonal XZ
  b) area of the rhombus
  c) angle WY makes with WX.

Q17 Two mountains are 1020 m and 1235 m high. Standing on the summit of the lower one I look up through an angle of elevation of 16° to see the summit of the higher one. Calculate the horizontal distance between the two mountains.

Q18 A girl is flying a kite. She holds the string, which is 45 m long, at a height of 1.3 m above the ground. The string of the kite makes an angle of 33° with the horizontal. What is the vertical height of the kite from the ground?

Q19 I am standing on top of an 80 m high tower. I look due north and see two cars with angles of depression of 38° and 49°. Calculate:
  a) how far each car is from the base of the tower
  b) how far apart the cars are.

Q20 A ship sails on a bearing of 300° for 100 km. The captain can then see a lighthouse due south of him that he knows is due west of his starting point. Calculate how far west the lighthouse is from the ship's starting point.

3D Pythagoras and Trigonometry

Q1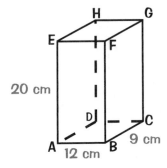

This rectangular box is 20 cm by 12 cm by 9 cm.
Calculate:
  a) angle ABE
  b) length AF
  c) length DF
  d) angle EBH.

Q2 This pyramid is on a square base of side 56 cm. Its vertical height is 32 cm. Calculate the length of:
  a) the line from E to the mid-point of BC
  b) the sloping edge BE.

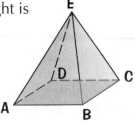

Q3 A rectangular box measures 20 cm by 30 cm by 8 cm.
Calculate the lengths of:
  a) the diagonal of each rectangular face
  b) the diagonal through the centre of the box.

Q4 This glass has a radius of 2.8 cm. The straw in the glass makes an angle of 70° with the base and protrudes 4 cm above the rim.
  a) How tall is the glass?
  b) How long is the straw?

Q5 A shop sells the three different gift boxes shown on the right. Katie wants to buy the cheapest box that will fit a pen that is 10 cm long. Which box should she buy?

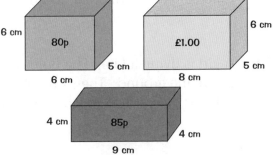

Q6 This cone has a perpendicular height of 9 cm.
The centre of the base is O. The slant line from X makes an angle of 23° with the central axis. Calculate:
  a) the radius of the base
  b) the area of the base
  c) the volume of the cone.

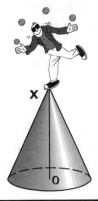

The Sine and Cosine Rules

Make sure you know the Sine Rule and <u>both forms</u> of the Cosine Rule.
The one to use depends on which angles and sides you're given.

Q1 Calculate the lengths required to 3 s.f.

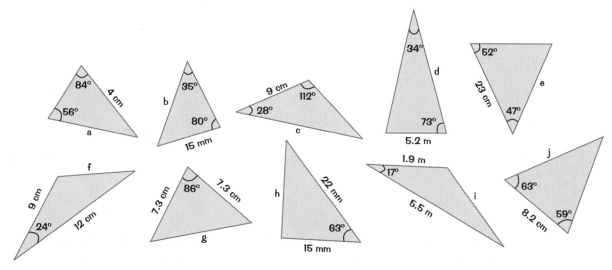

Q2 Calculate the angles required, to the nearest degree.

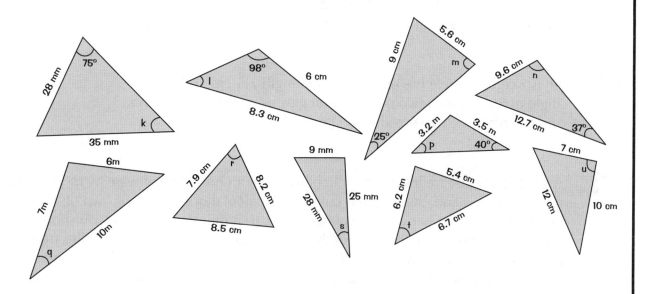

The Sine and Cosine Rules

Q3 Calculate the lettered sides and angles.

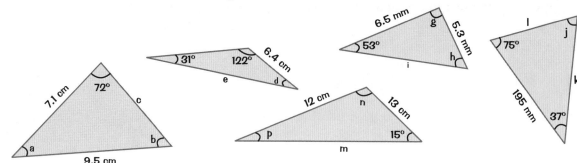

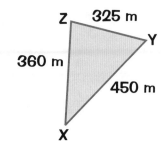

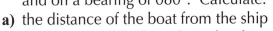

Q4 This field has measurements as shown. Calculate:

a) ∠ZXY

b) ∠XYZ

c) ∠YZX.

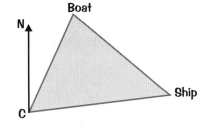

Q5 Peter is standing on a bridge over a river. He can see a tree on each bank, one 33 m and the other 35 m away from him. If he looks through an angle of 20° going from one tree to the other, how far apart are the two trees?

Q6 A coastguard sees a boat on a bearing of 038° from him and 25 km away. He also sees a ship 42 km away and on a bearing of 080°. Calculate:

a) the distance of the boat from the ship

b) the bearing of the boat from the ship.

Q7 An isosceles triangle has equal sides of length 7.5 cm and an angle of 56°. Sketch two possible triangles using this information and calculate the two possible lengths of the third side.

Q8 Air traffic control are testing the reliability of their computer software by monitoring two aeroplanes and checking the computer's calculations with their own. If the horizontal distance between the planes drops to 3 miles or less, an alarm should be triggered on the computer. One of the test planes is at a distance of 5 miles from the tower, and on a bearing of 020° from the tower. The second is at a distance of 4.6 miles on a bearing of 034° and the alarm is ringing. Calculate the horizontal distance between the planes and comment on the reliability of the software.

Q9 A parallelogram has sides of length 8 cm and 4.5 cm. One angle of the parallelogram is 124°. Calculate the lengths of the two diagonals.

The Sine and Cosine Rules

Q10 A vertical flagpole FP has two stay wires to the ground at A and B. They cannot be equidistant from P, as the ground is uneven. AB is 22 m, ∠PAB is 34° and ∠PBA is 50°. Calculate the distances:

a) PA

b) PB.

If A is level with P and the angle of elevation of F from A is 49°, calculate:

c) FA

d) PF.

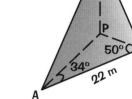

Q11 An aircraft leaves A and flies 257 km to B on a bearing of 257°. It then flies on to C, 215 km away on a bearing of 163° from B. Calculate:

a) ∠ABC

b) distance CA

c) the bearing needed to fly from A direct to C.

Q12 On my clock the hour hand is 5.5 cm, the minute hand 8 cm and the second hand 7 cm, measured from the centre. Calculate the distance between the tips of the:

a) hour and minute hands at 10 o'clock

b) minute and second hands 15 seconds before 20 past the hour

c) hour and minute hands at 1020.

So the minute hand is at 19.75 minutes past the hour.

Q13 A surveyor wants to measure the height of a building. She measures the angle of elevation of the top of the building from the two different positions shown. Calculate the height of the building to the nearest metre.

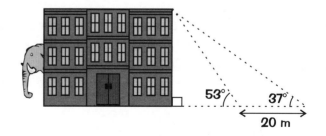

Q14 Mary and Jane were standing one behind the other, 2.3 m apart, each holding one of the two strings of a kite flying directly in front of them. The angles of elevation of the kite from the girls were 65° and 48° respectively. Assuming the ends of both strings are held at the same height above the ground, calculate the length of each string.

114

Sin, Cos and Tan for Larger Angles

Q1   Calculate the lettered sides and angles.

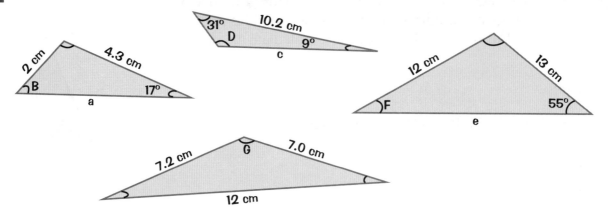

Q2   If $90° < x < 180°$, find x when:

a) $\sin x = 0.84$ **b)** $\sin x = 0.173$ **c)** $\tan x = -1$ **d)** $\tan x = -14.3$

Q3   Fayrmin looks upon a mystical glade. In the glade is a unicorn being guarded by 2 minotaurs. One minotaur is 23 metres from the unicorn and the other one is 14 metres from the unicorn. They stand either side of the unicorn at an angle of 118°. How far apart are the minotaurs?

Q4   Adam surveys a building from inside. He finds the angle between the floor and the front is 58°. He walks to the other end of the building, where the roof meets the floor, and finds the angle between them to be 13°. The distance from one end of the building to the other is 120 m. Calculate:

a) the angle between the front of the building and the roof

b) the length of the building front and roof

c) the height of the highest point of the building.

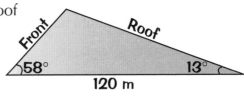

Q5   A sailor sees a storm in the distance. The sailor knows that an island is 7 kilometres away from the boat and calculates that the angle between this island and the storm is 94° and that there is 26 kilometres of water between the storm and the island.
Calculate the proximity of the ship to the storm.

Q6   PQR is a triangle. The size of angle P is 25°.
Side r is 12 m long and side p is 7.5 m long.
What are the two possible values of the size of angle R?

Q7   A spacecraft (S) is travelling to the moon. When it is 210 000 km from mission control on Earth (E) it is found to be 170 000 km away from the landing site at the moon base (M). The straight-line distance between mission control and the moon base is 370 000 km. Calculate the angle ESM. Give your answer to 1 d.p.

Mean, Median, Mode and Range

For finding the <u>mode</u> and <u>median</u> put the data in order of size — it's much easier to find the most frequent and middle values that way.

The <u>mean</u> involves a bit more calculation, but hey, you're doing maths...

Q1 The local rugby team scored the following number of tries in their first 10 matches of the season:

3	5	4	2	0	1	3	0	3	4

Find their modal number of tries.

Q2 Find the mean, median, mode and range of these numbers:

1	2	–2	0	1	8	3	–3	2	4	–2	2

Q3 A company has 9 employees in the sales department who earn commission. They are advertising for another salesperson and want to say in the advert how much commission their staff earn on average. The amount of commission the 9 existing salespeople earned last year is as follows:

£13,000	£9,000	£7,500
£18,000	£12,000	£7,500
£23,000	£15,000	£11,500

a) Find the mean, median and mode of their earnings.
b) Which one does not give a good indication of their average commission?
c) Which should the company put in the advert, and why?

Q4 Molly is writing a letter of complaint to the bus company because she thinks her bus to school is regularly late. Over 3 weeks, Molly kept a record of how many minutes her bus was either early or late, and put this in her letter. (She used + for late and – for early.)

+2	–1	0	+5	–4
–7	0	–8	0	+4
–4	–3	+14	+2	0

a) Calculate the mean lateness/earliness of the bus.
b) Calculate the median.
c) What is the mode?
d) The bus company use the answers to **a)**, **b)** and **c)** to claim they are always on time. Is this true?

Careful with this — you have to use the averages to find the total weight, then divide to find the new average.

Q5 The average weight of the 11 players in a football team was 72.5 kg. The average weight of the 5 reserve players was 75.6 kg. What was the average weight of the whole squad? (Give your answer to 3 s.f.)

Q6 The mean daily weight of potatoes sold in a greengrocer's from Monday to Friday was 14 kg. The mean daily weight of potatoes sold from Monday to Saturday was 15 kg. How many kg of potatoes were sold on Saturday?

Mean, Median, Mode and Range

Q7   Colin averaged 83% over 3 exams. His average for the first two exams was 76%.
What was Colin's score in the final exam?

Q8   The range for a certain list of numbers is 26, and one of the numbers in the list is 48.
   a) What is the lowest possible value a number in the list could be?
   b) What is the highest possible value that could be in the list?

Q9   An ordinary dice is rolled 6 times, landing on a different number each time.
   a) What is the mean score?
   b) What is the median score?
   c) What is the range of scores?

Q10   The bar graph shows the amount of time Jim and Bob spend
watching TV during the week.

   a) Find the mean amount of time per
   day each spends watching TV.

   b) Find the range of times for each of
   them.

   c) Using your answers from **a)** and **b)**,
   comment on what you notice about
   the way they watch TV.

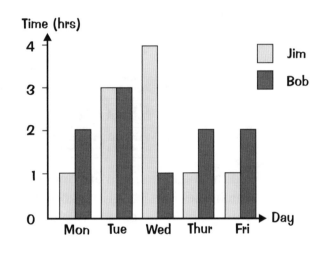

Q11   Mr Jones posted 88 Christmas cards first class on
Monday. His friends received them over the week:
40 on Tuesday, 28 on Wednesday, 9 on Thursday,
6 on Friday and the remainder on Saturday.
   a) Find the modal number of days it took for the cards
   to arrive.
   b) Find the median number of days it took for the cards
   to arrive.
   c) "The majority of first class post arrives within 2
   days." Is the above statement true or false in the
   light of the data?

Q12   In each of the following cases, decide which average is referred to:
   a) this average is least appropriate when the total number of values is small
   b) this average is least affected if one of the values is removed at random
   c) this average is most affected by the presence of extreme values.

Frequency Tables

You've got to be able to do these in both row and
column form, because they could give you either one.
There's no real difference, and the rules are still the same.

Q1 To monitor their annual performance, a travel company logs all calls to their sales desk.
The number of calls per day received by the sales desk over a given year are shown here.

No. of Calls	10	11	12	13	14	15	16 and over
No. of Days	110	70	120	27	18	12	8

a) Find the median number of calls.
b) Find the modal number of calls.

Q2 A student has classes in Mathematics (M),
English (E), French (F), Art (A) and Science (S).
Her timetable is shown opposite.

Monday	S S E E A
Tuesday	E M M A A
Wednesday	S M E F F
Thursday	F E E A S
Friday	M M E S S

a) Complete the following frequency table for a week's lessons:

b) Calculate the number of French
lessons that the student will attend
during a 12-week term.

Subject	M	E	F	A	S
Frequency					

c) What is the modal lesson?

Q3 20 pupils are asked to estimate the length (to the nearest m) of their gardens.
Here are the results: 10, 8, 6, 4, 10, 8, 0, 14, 12, 8, 10, 6, 1, 6, 10, 8, 6, 6, 8, 8
Copy the frequency table below and put the estimates in.

a) Find the mode of the data.
b) Find the median of the data.
c) State the range of the data.

Length (m)	4 and under	6	8	10	12	14 and over
Frequency						

Frequency Tables

Q4 130 female bus drivers were weighed to the nearest 5 kg.

a) Find the median weight.
b) Find the modal weight.
c) Complete the table and use it to estimate the mean weight.

Weight (to nearest 5 kg) (kg)	Frequency	Weight × Frequency
50	40	
55	30	
60	45	
65	10	
70	5	

Q5 A football magazine rates teams according to how many goals they're likely to score in a match, based on their last 20 matches. The table below shows the number of goals scored by Spark Bridge Wanderers over this period.

No. of goals	0	1	2	3	4	5	6
Frequency	0	1	1	7	6	3	2

Find the mean, mode and median of the data.

Q6 A tornado has struck the hamlet of Moose-on-the-Wold. Many houses have had windows broken. The frequency table shows the devastating effects.

No. of windows broken per house	0	1	2	3	4	5	6
Frequency	5	3	4	11	13	7	2

a) Calculate the modal number of broken windows.
b) Calculate the median number of broken windows.
c) Calculate the mean number of broken windows.

Q7 Using the computerised till in a shoe shop, the manager can predict what stock to order from the previous week's sales.
Opposite is the tabulated printout for <u>last week</u> for <u>men's shoes</u>.

Shoe size	5	6	7	8	9	10	11
frequency	9	28	56	70	56	28	9

a) The mean, mode and median for this data can be compared. For each of the following statements decide whether it is true or false.
  i) The <u>mode</u> for this data is <u>70</u>.
  ii) The <u>mean</u> is <u>greater than</u> the <u>median</u> for this distribution.
  iii) The mean, median and mode are <u>all equal</u> in this distribution.

b) What <u>percentage</u> of customers bought shoes of the <u>mean size</u> from last week's sales data:

  i) 30%   ii) 70%   iii) 0.273%   or   iv) 27.3%?

Grouped Frequency Tables

Q1 The speeds of 32 skiers at a certain corner of a downhill course are tabulated below.

Speed (km/h)	$40 \leq s < 45$	$45 \leq s < 50$	$50 \leq s < 55$	$55 \leq s < 60$	$60 \leq s < 65$
Frequency	4	8	10	7	3
Mid-Interval					
Frequency × Mid-Interval					

a) By completing the frequency table, estimate the mean speed.
b) How many skiers were travelling at less than 55 km/h?
c) How many skiers were travelling at 50 km/h or faster?

Q2 The weights in kg of 18 newly felled trees are noted below:

272.7 333.2 251.0 246.5 328.0 259.6 200.2 312.8 344.3
226.8 362.0 348.3 256.1 232.9 309.7 398.0 284.5 327.4

a) Complete the frequency table.

Weight (kg)	Tally	Frequency	Mid-Interval	Frequency × Mid-Interval
$200 \leq w < 250$				
$250 \leq w < 300$				
$300 \leq w < 350$				
$350 \leq w < 400$				

b) Estimate the mean weight using the frequency table.
c) What is the modal group?

Q3 48 numbers are recorded below:

0.057 0.805 0.056 0.979 0.419 0.160 0.534 0.763
0.642 0.569 0.773 0.055 0.349 0.892 0.664 0.136
0.528 0.792 0.085 0.546 0.549 0.908 0.639 0.000
0.614 0.478 0.421 0.472 0.292 0.579 0.542 0.356
0.070 0.890 0.883 0.333 0.033 0.323 0.544 0.668
0.094 0.049 0.049 0.999 0.632 0.700 0.983 0.356

a) Transfer the data into the frequency table.

Number	$0 \leq n < 0.2$	$0.2 \leq n < 0.4$	$0.4 \leq n < 0.6$	$0.6 \leq n < 0.8$	$0.8 \leq n < 1$
Tally					
Frequency					
Mid-Interval					
Frequency × Mid-Interval					

b) Write down the modal class(es).
c) Which group contains the median?
d) Estimate the mean value.

Quartiles and the Interquartile Range

Remember to put the data in <u>ascending</u> order before you work out where the quartiles come in a list.

Q1 The weights (in g) of 29 eggs are:

60	72	58	60	68	69	59	72	54	56	65	68	63	70	71
67	64	63	69	62	63	67	59	72	61	66		65	67	70

a) What is the median?
b) Which quartile is equivalent to the median?

Q2 The following table shows the number of cars parked in a multi-storey car park at midday on each day in December:

690	720	580	590	210	650	640	710
700	750	790	220	790	840	830	820
900	880	480	1000	990	1020	1010	1000
80	240	370	510	460	600	580	

a) What is the range?
b) What is the lower quartile, Q_1?
c) What is the median?
d) What is the upper quartile, Q_3?

Quartiles divide the data into 4 equal groups.

Q3 For all the whole numbers from 1 to 399 inclusive:

What is the interquartile range?

The interquartile range tells you the range of the middle 50% of the data.

Q4 The range of 99 different integers is 98, and the median is 350.

a) What is the lower quartile, Q_1?
b) What is the interquartile range?

Cumulative Frequency

Q1 Using the cumulative frequency curve,
find the:

a) median

b) lower quartile

c) upper quartile

d) interquartile range.

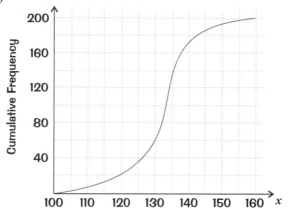

Q2 The number of passengers using a bus service each day has been recorded over a
4-week period. The data is presented in the table below:

No. passengers	$0 \leq n < 50$	$50 \leq n < 100$	$100 \leq n < 150$	$150 \leq n < 200$	$200 \leq n < 250$	$250 \leq n < 300$
Frequency	2	7	10	5	3	1
Cumulative Frequency						
Mid-Interval						
Frequency × Mid-Interval						

A mean passenger

a) By completing the table, estimate the mean number of passengers.

b) By plotting a cumulative frequency curve, determine the median value.

c) What is the modal group?

With cumulative frequency you always
plot the highest value from each class.

Q3 40 pupils have taken an exam and their marks are recorded in a frequency table.

Mark (%)	$0 \leq m < 20$	$20 \leq m < 40$	$40 \leq m < 60$	$60 \leq m < 80$	$80 \leq m < 100$
Frequency	2	12	18	5	3
Cumulative Frequency					

a) Complete the table and plot the cumulative frequency curve.

b) What is the value of the lower quartile?

c) What is the interquartile range?

d) What is the median mark?

Cumulative Frequency

Q4 One hundred scores for a board game are presented in the table below.

Score	$31 \leq s < 41$	$41 \leq s < 51$	$51 \leq s < 61$	$61 \leq s < 71$	$71 \leq s < 81$	$81 \leq s < 91$	$91 \leq s < 101$
Frequency	4	12	21	32	19	8	4
Cumulative Frequency							

a) What is the modal group?
b) Which group contains the median score?
c) By plotting the cumulative frequency curve estimate the value of the median score.
d) Find the interquartile range.

Q5 The following frequency table gives the distribution of the lives of electric bulbs.

a) Complete the frequency table.

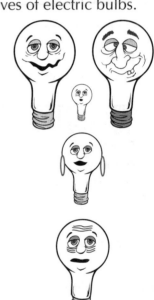

Life (hours)	Frequency	Cumulative Frequency
$900 \leq L < 1000$	10	
$1000 \leq L < 1100$	12	
$1100 \leq L < 1200$	15	
$1200 \leq L < 1300$	18	
$1300 \leq L < 1400$	22	
$1400 \leq L < 1500$	17	
$1500 \leq L < 1600$	14	
$1600 \leq L < 1700$	9	

b) Which group contains the median value?
c) By drawing the cumulative frequency curve, estimate the value of the median.
d) Determine values for the upper and lower quartiles.

Q6 30 pupils recorded the time taken (minutes : seconds) to boil some water.
Here are their results:

2:37 2:37 3:17 3:30 2:45 2:13 3:18 3:12 3:38 3:29
3:04 3:24 4:13 3:01 3:11 2:33 3:37 4:24 3:59 3:11
3:22 3:13 2:57 3:12 3:07 4:17 3:31 3:42 3:51 3:24

a) By using a tally, transfer the data into the frequency table.
b) Draw the cumulative frequency curve.

Time	$2:00 \leq t < 2:30$	$2:30 \leq t < 3:00$	$3:00 \leq t < 3:30$	$3:30 \leq t < 4:00$	$4:00 \leq t < 4:30$
Tally					
Frequency					
Cumulative Frequency					

c) Using your graph, read off the median and the upper and lower quartiles.
d) What is the interquartile range?

Pie Charts

Everyone loves a pie chart. Oh, no, sorry, that's pies...

When constructing a pie chart, follow the three steps:

1) Add up the numbers for each sector to get the <u>TOTAL</u>.
2) Divide 360° by the <u>TOTAL</u> to get the <u>MULTIPLIER</u>.
3) Multiply <u>EVERY</u> number by the <u>MULTIPLIER</u> to get the <u>ANGLE</u> of each <u>SECTOR</u>.

Q1 A company that makes and sells pies wants to add a nutritional information diagram to their packaging. <u>Construct a pie chart</u> using the template on the right, to show the following nutritional data for one of their pies:

Contents of Pie	Amount per 100 g
Carbohydrate	35 g
Protein	15 g
Fat	10 g
Magical fairy dust	40 g

Q2 According to the tourist board for the Hindle Isles, 380 000 people visited the biggest island in the group, Sherrington, in 2009. The <u>distribution</u> of tourists for the <u>whole group of islands</u> is shown in the pie chart. Find the number of tourists visiting each of the other islands in 2009. Round each number to the nearest 10 000.

Use the info you're given to find the number of tourists represented by 1° by measuring the pie chart with a protractor.

The distribution of visitors to the Hindle Isles in 2009

Q3 The pie chart shows the results of a survey of forty 11-year-olds when asked what their <u>favourite vegetable</u> is with Sunday lunch. Which one of the following may be <u>deduced</u> from the information in the <u>pie chart</u>?

a) Potatoes are the <u>least popular</u> vegetable.
b) 3/4 of the children <u>like potatoes</u> of some type.
c) 1/10 of the children like <u>carrots or cauliflower</u>.
d) 11/40 of the children asked what their favourite vegetable is, replied "<u>Don't eat vegetables</u>."

Q4 The pie charts opposite appear in a newspaper article about favourite pies. Nicki says that more women like apple pies than men.

Comment on <u>whether it's possible</u> to tell this from the pie charts.

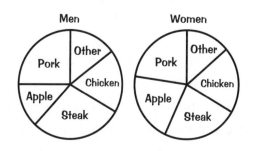

More Graphs and Charts

Q1 This bar chart shows the marks from a test done by some students:

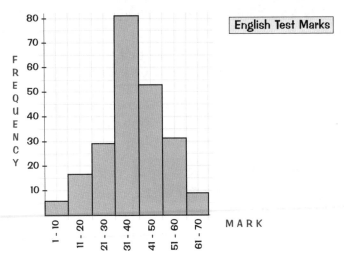

English Test Marks

a) How many students scored 20 marks or less?

b) The pass mark for this test was 31.
   How many students passed the test?

c) How many students took the test?

Q2 The local library is carrying out a survey to find the amount of time people spend reading each day. Complete the frequency table below and then draw a bar chart to show the results.

Time spent reading (mins)	Tally	Frequency
1 - 15	ⵔⵔⵔ l	6
16 - 30	ⵔⵔⵔ lll	
31 - 45	lll	
46 - 60	ⵔⵔⵔ	
61 - 75	lll	

Q3 This pictogram shows the favourite drinks of a group of pupils.

Favourite Drinks	Number of Pupils
Lemonade	✦ ✦ ✦ ✦ ✦ ✦ ✦ ✦ ✦
Cola	✦ ✦ ✦ ✦ ✦ ✦ ✦ ✦ ✦ ✦
Cherryade	✦ ✦ ✦ ✦ ✦ ✦
Orange Squash	✦ ✦ ✦
Milk	✦

✦ Represents 2 pupils.

a) How many pupils were questioned?

b) How many pupils prefer either milk or orange squash?

c) 18 pupils liked lemonade best. How many more liked cola best?

d) Comment on the popularity of cola compared with milk.

Histograms and Dispersion

It's the <u>size that counts</u>... You've got to look at the <u>area</u> of the bars to find the frequency. That means looking at the <u>width</u> as well as the height.

Q1 The Bog Snorkelling Appreciation Society conducts a survey on the ages of all their members. The histogram below shows the age distribution of the people surveyed. The Society organises a 'Seniors' bog snorkelling event for members aged 60 or older. Use the graph to estimate the maximum number of people that might take part.

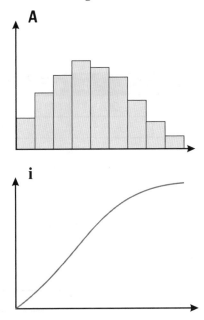

Use the key to work out the frequencies.

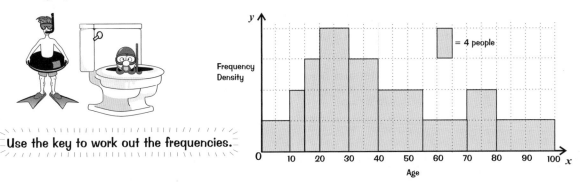

Q2 The weight of honey collected from several beehives is tabulated below.
a) Complete the frequency table by calculating the frequency densities.
b) Draw a histogram to represent this data.
c) Use your histogram to estimate the number of beehives that produced more than 6 kg of honey.

Weight (kg)	$0 \leq w < 2$	$2 \leq w < 4$	$4 \leq w < 7$	$7 \leq w < 9$	$9 \leq w < 15$
Frequency	3	2	6	9	12
Frequency density					

Q3 Match the histograms to their corresponding cumulative frequency curves.

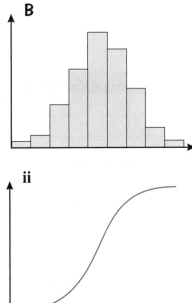

Histograms and Dispersion

Know your shapes — they're bound to ask you what different-shaped graphs mean, so get learning.

Q4 A group of sixth formers took part in a survey to see how much time they spent watching TV each week.

a) Complete the table by filling in the frequency density column.
b) How many students took part in the survey?
c) Represent the data as a histogram.
d) Estimate the number of students that watch more than 7, but less than 13 hours each week.

No. of hours	Frequency	Frequency density
$0 \leq h < 1$	6	
$1 \leq h < 3$	13	
$3 \leq h < 5$	15	
$5 \leq h < 8$	9	
$8 \leq h < 10$	23	
$10 \leq h < 15$	25	
$15 \leq h < 20$	12	

Q5 Below are two histograms — one shows the weights of a sample of 16-year-olds, and the other shows the weights of a sample of 1 kg bags of sugar. Say which is which.

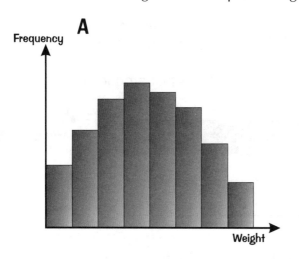

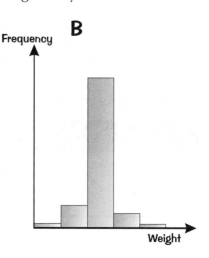

Q6 A local newspaper employee has collected data on the salaries of 100 people living in the area. His data is shown in the table below.

Salary (£1000s)	$0 \leq s < 10$	$10 \leq s < 20$	$20 \leq s < 30$	$30 \leq s < 40$	$40 \leq s < 50$
Frequency	10	25	42	20	3
Frequency Density					

a) Complete the table and draw a histogram to show the data.
b) The newspaper prints this histogram alongside the one shown on the right. It represents data from an identical survey done 10 years earlier. Write a comment comparing current salaries and those from 10 years ago.

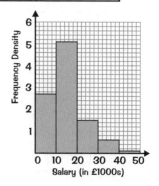

Histograms and Dispersion

Q7 A farmer keeps track of the amount of milk produced by his cows each day.

Amount of Milk (Litres)	Frequency	Frequency Density	Mid-Interval	Frequency × Mid-Interval
0 ⩽ M < 1	6			
1 ⩽ M < 5	6			
5 ⩽ M < 8	6			
8 ⩽ M < 10	6			
10 ⩽ M < 15	6			
15 ⩽ M < 20	6			

a) Complete the frequency table.
b) Use the mid-interval technique to estimate the mean.
c) Draw a histogram to show the data.
d) On how many days is less than 12.5 litres produced?

Q8 The publishers of a teen magazine want to increase its price.
To help them choose the best price, they carried out a survey of
188 readers to see how much pocket money they receive each week.

Amount (£)	Frequency	Frequency Density	Mid-Interval	Frequency × Mid-Interval
0 ≤ A < 0.50	11			
0.50 ≤ A < 1.00	25			
1.00 ≤ A < 1.30	9			
1.30 ≤ A < 1.50	12			
1.50 ≤ A < 1.80	24			
1.80 ≤ A < 2.50	21			
2.50 ≤ A < 3.10	54			
3.10 ≤ A < 4.10	32			

a) By first completing the table, estimate the mean amount of pocket money.
b) What is the modal class?

   The publishers decide that £1.40 would be a reasonable price, but they want to check
   that at least 75% of readers could afford to buy the magazine with their pocket money.

c) Draw a histogram of the data and estimate how many readers receive less than £1.40.
d) According to your estimate, do 75% of readers receive £1.40 or more?

Probability

Probability can be a bit of a struggle — here's a quick reminder of the basics...

PROBABILITIES are always between 0 and 1

1) You should express probabilities as a <u>fraction</u> or a <u>decimal</u>.
2) A probability of <u>ZERO</u> means that it will <u>definitely not</u> happen.
3) A probability of <u>ONE</u> means it will <u>definitely</u> happen.

Q1 The number line opposite is a <u>probability scale</u>. Place the letters where you think the following statements lie, in terms of the <u>chance</u> of the event happening.

0   ½   1

a) The probability of getting a <u>head</u> on a toss of a 10p piece.
b) The probability of <u>choosing a red ball</u> at random from a bag containing 2 red balls and 1 green ball.
c) The probability of shaking a <u>five</u> on an ordinary dice.
d) The probability of choosing a <u>Guatemalan stamp</u> from a bag containing 60 British stamps and 40 French stamps.

Q2 Debbie's employer organises a weekly prize draw, where the winning employee is selected at random. Debbie only joins in if her chance of winning is at least 0.1. If there are 8 other people playing this week, will Debbie choose to play?

SHORTHAND NOTATION

1) <u>P(x) = 0.25</u> simply means "the probability of event x happening is 0.25".
2) E.g.: if you roll a dice, the <u>probability of rolling a 6</u> will be written as <u>P(6)</u>.

Q3 After <u>49 tosses</u> of an unbiased coin, 24 have been heads and 25 have been tails. What is <u>P(50th toss will be a head)</u>?

Q4 If the probability of picking a banana from a fruit bowl is <u>0.27</u>, what is the probability of picking something which is <u>not</u> a banana?

Q5 A bag contains <u>3 red</u> balls, <u>4 blue</u> balls and <u>5 green</u> balls. A ball is chosen at random from the bag. What is the probability that:
a) it is green   b) it is blue   c) it is red   d) it is <u>not</u> red?

Q6 Students at school conduct a survey of the <u>colours</u> of parents' cars, where every parent owns one car. The table shows the results.

Red	Blue	Yellow	White	Green	Other
40	29	13	20	16	14

a) What is the probability of a parent owning a <u>red</u> car?
b) What is the probability of a parent owning a car that is <u>not</u> blue <u>or</u> green?

Q7 The probability of it raining during the monsoon is ¾, on a particular day.
a) What is the probability of it <u>not raining</u>?
b) If a monsoon 'season' lasts approximately <u>100 days</u>, how many days are likely to be <u>dry</u>?

Probability

Q8 The students in a class were asked what their favourite type of pizza was. The table below shows the results.

Pepperoni	Ham and pineapple	Ham and mushroom	Margarita	Other
6	11	5	3	5

If a student is picked at random from the class, what is the probability that:

a) their favourite type of pizza is ham and pineapple

b) their favourite type of pizza is pepperoni

c) their favourite type of pizza is not margarita?

Q9 a) What is the probability of randomly selecting either a black Ace or black King from an ordinary pack of playing cards?

b) If the entire suit of clubs is removed from a pack of cards, what is the probability of randomly selecting a red 7 from the remaining cards?

c) If all the 7s are then removed from the remaining cards, what is the probability of randomly selecting the 4 of diamonds?

Remember the OR rule — P(A or B) = P(A) + P(B).

Q10 For the spinner shown, the probability of the ball landing on each of the numbers is listed in the table below.

Number	1	2	3	4	5	6
Probability	$\frac{1}{6}$	$\frac{1}{3}$	$\frac{1}{6}$	$\frac{1}{12}$	$\frac{1}{12}$	$\frac{1}{6}$

a) Find the probability of landing on an even number.

b) What is the probability of landing on black?

c) Why is the probability of landing on a white or a 3 not $\frac{5}{12} + \frac{1}{6}$?

Q11 The wheel on the right is a game based on luck at a funfair. The wheel is spun and the player wins whatever the arrow lands on. If the arrow lands on lose, they win nothing. The wheel is unbiased and all the sections are the same size.

a) What is the probability of losing?

b) What is the probability of winning more than £3?

c) What is the probability of winning £1 or £2?

d) What is the probability of losing, or winning £5?

Probability

Q12 An ordinary coin is flipped, and then an unbiased 6-sided dice is rolled.

    a) List all the possible outcomes.

    b) What is the probability of:

        i) rolling a 5 on the dice

        ii) the outcome being a head and a 2

        iii) the outcome being a tail and at least a 3?

    c) If the dice is rolled 42 times, how many times would you expect it to be a 6?

Q13 The sample space diagram below shows all the possible outcomes of rolling a fair dice and spinning an unbiased spinner. Use the diagram to find out the probability of:

	Blue	Yellow	Green
1	1B	1Y	1G
2	2B	2Y	2G
3	3B	3Y	3G
4	4B	4Y	4G
5	5B	5Y	5G
6	6B	6Y	6G

    a) the spinner landing on green

    b) the spinner landing on blue or green, and the dice landing on a 5.

    c) the spinner landing on green or yellow and the dice landing on a number less than 4?

Q14 There are 2 unbiased spinners: one with 3 sides numbered 1, 2, 3, and the other with 7 sides numbered 1, 2, 3, 4, 5, 6, 7.

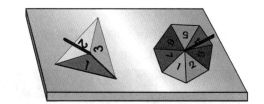

    a) If both are spun together, list all the possible outcomes.

    b) Complete the following table showing the sum of the 2 numbers for each outcome.

	1	2	3	4	5	6	7
1							
2							
3							

    c) What is the probability that the sum is 6?

    d) What is the probability that the sum is even?

    e) What is the probability that the sum is greater than or equal to 8?

    f) What is the probability that the sum is less than 8?

    g) Explain how you can work out the probability in part **f)** without using the table.

Probability — Expected and Relative Frequency

Q1 **a)** A biased dice is rolled 40 times. A six came up 14 times.
Calculate the relative frequency that a six was rolled.

b) The same dice is rolled another 60 times. From this, a six came up 24 times.
Calculate the relative frequency that a six was rolled.

c) Use the data from **a)** and **b)** to make the best estimate you can
of the probability of rolling a six with the dice.

d) What is the expected frequency of sixes if the dice is rolled eight times?

Q2 The notepad below shows orders for 4 different sorts of rice at a certain Indian
restaurant. Based on this data, what is the probability that the next order of rice is:

a) for pilau rice?

b) for spicy mushroom or special fried rice?

c) not for boiled rice?

*If you're asked to work out probabilities based on
some data, it's a **relative frequency** question.*

boiled	20
pilau	24
spicy mushroom	10
special fried	6

Q3 Charlton is making a bet with his friend
before the local cricket team play a match.
He thinks the match will end in a draw.
A local newspaper prints the team's results
over their last 20 matches, as shown.

W	W	L	D	D	W	W	L	W	L
D	L	L	D	W	D	W	W	L	L

a) Complete the frequency table.

b) Charlton reasons that since there are 3
possible results for any match, the probability
that the next match will be drawn (D) is $\frac{1}{3}$.
Explain why Charlton is wrong.

Outcome	Frequency
W	
D	
L	

c) Suggest a value for the probability of a draw based on the team's past performance.

d) Based on their past performance, are the team most likely to win, lose, or draw?

Q4 Kenny has written a random number generating computer program, Numbertron 5000.
He thinks a bug has made the program biased towards odd numbers.
He tests it by making it pick a number from 1 to 10. He does this 80 times.
If the program is really random, how many times in 80 trials would you expect it to pick:

a) 4?   **b)** an odd number?

Here are the results of Kenny's experiment:

Number	1	2	3	4	5	6	7	8	9	10
No. of times picked	7	7	9	8	10	7	9	6	8	9

c) What is the relative frequency of Numbertron 5000 picking an odd number?

d) If the program is truly random, what would you expect to happen to the relative
frequency of each number if Kenny repeated the experiment with 100 000 trials?

SECTION SEVEN — STATISTICS

Probability — Tree Diagrams

Q1 3 balls are drawn at random, without replacement, from a bag containing 4 green balls and 3 red balls.

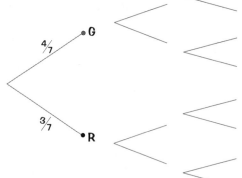

a) Complete the tree diagram to the right showing all the possible outcomes and their probabilities.
b) What is the probability that exactly 2 green balls are drawn?
c) What is the probability that the last ball drawn is the same colour as the first?

> For AND you MULTIPLY along the branches.
> For OR you ADD the end results.

Q2 How many times must you roll an ordinary 6-sided dice for the probability of getting at least one 6 to be more than 0.5?

> Don't forget the "at least" trick —
> P(at least 1 six) = 1 – P(no sixes).

Q3 An unbiased dice in the shape of a tetrahedron has vertices numbered 1, 2, 3, 4. To win a game with this dice, you must throw a 4. At each go you have a maximum of 3 attempts.
a) Using a tree diagram, calculate the probability of winning with the second throw of the first go.
b) What is the probability of winning on the first go?

Q4 3 coins are drawn at random, without replacement, from a piggy bank containing 7 pound coins and 4 twenty-pence pieces.
a) Draw a tree diagram showing all possible outcomes and their probabilities.
b) Find the probability that the first coin selected is different in value from the third.
c) Find the probability that less than £1.50 is drawn altogether.

Q5 Fabrizio is practising taking penalties. The probability that he misses the goal completely is $\frac{1}{8}$. The probability that the goalkeeper saves the penalty is $\frac{3}{8}$. The probability that he scores is $\frac{1}{2}$. Fabrizio takes two penalties.

a) Calculate the probability that Fabrizio fails to score with his two penalties.
b) Calculate the probability that he scores only one goal.
c) Calculate the probability that Fabrizio scores on neither or both of his 2 attempts.

Q6 Trevor and his 2 brothers and 5 friends are seated at random in a row of 8 seats at the cinema. What is the probability that Trevor has one brother on his immediate left and one on his immediate right?

> Careful here — you have to include the probability
> that Trevor sits in one of the six middle seats.

Drawing a tree diagram might be a bit of a faff, but it can really help to make the question clearer. So if you're stuck, give the old tree diagram a try.

MEWI42